Zeloof-Stuart

Geoffrey Marks is a medical writer and was associate editor of *Physicians Management*.

Fabian Bachrach

William K. Beatty is librarian and professor of medical bibliography at Northwestern University Medical School, Evanston, Illinois.

WOMEN
IN WHITE

WOMEN
IN WHITE

Geoffrey Marks and
William K. Beatty

Illustrated

CHARLES SCRIBNER'S SONS • NEW YORK

3 5 7 9 11 13 15 17 19 H/C 20 18 16 14 12 10 8 6 4 2

Printed in the United States of America
Library of Congress Catalog Card Number 70–38281
SBN 684–12843–8 (cloth)

FOR
Thomas J. Nickel, R.N.

Contents

PART THREE: WOMEN
IN RELATED FIELDS

A Portfolio
of Pictures

Hygeia, daughter of Aesculapius and goddess of health

12

OPPOSITE: *The Aesculapian hospital at Epidaurus, with sacred serpent in attendance*

Medicine chest used by the Egyptian Queen Mentuhotep (c.2500 B.C.)

13

14

OPPOSITE, TOP: *Agnodice (c.300 B.C.), who practiced medicine disguised as a man and then won the right to practice in women's clothing*

OPPOSITE, BOTTOM: *Trotula, the first outstanding woman teacher of medicine in the Christian era*

BELOW: *Hildegard of Bingen, a practical visionary*

Louyse Bourgeois, aggressive French midwife (c.1600) who delivered royal infants as well as babies of the poor

Marie-Louise Lachapelle, a leading French midwife (c.1800) who handled and described 40,000 deliveries

Dr. James Barry, the military masquerader

OPPOSITE, TOP: *Dr. Elizabeth Blackwell, pioneer medical student and champion of women in medicine*

OPPOSITE, BOTTOM: *Dr. Emily Blackwell, pioneer medical teacher and administrator*

*"Dr. Zak"—Marie E. Zakrzewska, Polish midwife who
came to the United States to obtain her medical degree*

The New York Infirmary for Women and Children—initiated, funded, and run by Elizabeth and Emily Blackwell and Marie Zakrzewska

22

OPPOSITE: *Dr. Elizabeth Garrett Anderson, pioneer in opening the profession of medicine to English women*

Dr. Ann Preston, member of the first graduating class, and later dean, of the Woman's Medical College of Pennsylvania

Dr. Sophia Jex-Blake, English firebrand in the struggle for women's rights in medicine

Anna Morandi Mahzolini, who introduced new methods into the teaching of anatomy

Dr. Mary Putnam Jacobi, who broke down the prejudice against women at the University of Paris

OPPOSITE: *The Grand Amphitheatre, School of Surgery, University of Paris*

Dr. Emily Dunning, New York's first woman ambulance surgeon, in front of Gouverneur Hospital

OPPOSITE: *Dr. Alice Hamilton, humanitarian crusader in industrial medicine*

Florence Nightingale, politician, administrator, and nurse

Dorothea Lynde Dix, champion of the insane

BELOW: *Pennsylvania State Lunatic Hospital at Harrisburg, one of the concrete results of Dorothea Dix's lifelong crusade*

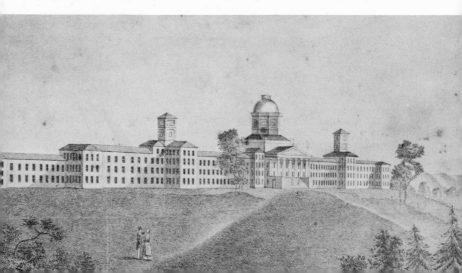

Jane Addams, founder of Hull-House

Marie Curie, whose perseverance resulted in the discovery of radium

PART ONE

From Gods to Midwives

1. Ancient Healers—
Real and Legendary

"I swear by Apollo Physician and Asclepius and Hygieia and Panaceia and all the gods and goddesses"—these are the opening words of the Hippocratic oath customarily taken by doctors as they enter the practice of medicine.[1] In Greek mythology, Apollo, son of Zeus, had many roles. He was god of light, truth, and law, and the archer god who loosed deadly arrows against the powers of evil; he was also the beneficial healer who, through his oracle at Delphi, served as an intermediary between man and his gods.

AESCULAPIUS

The origin of Aesculapius (or Asclepius) has many versions. Some early legends claim he was semi-divine, others that he was mortal. Most agree that his father was Apollo and his mother the maiden Coronis, who, according to Hesiod, a Greek poet of the eighth century B.C., was the daughter of a king. It is generally believed that Aesculapius was delivered by the chief midwife of the gods, Eileithyia, around 1300 B.C., on Mount Titthion, above Epidauros in southern Greece—though the modern Dutch art historian J. Schouten speaks of the "feat of Apollo in the delivery of the baby Asklepias, namely by caesarean section, hence by surgical intervention."[2]

Whether Coronis was unfaithful to Apollo and was therefore killed by Artemis, his twin sister, or whether Apollo himself killed

Coronis accidentally, or whether she simply went off with another mortal, she disappears from the legends. Apollo turned the infant over to Cheiron, a legendary physician famous for his knowledge of herbs, to be brought up.

Even the birthplace of Aesculapius is not certain. The Greek poet Homer (who probably lived around 850 B.C.) placed it in Thessaly in northern Greece. He considered Aesculapius mortal, "the blameless physician," and recorded that his sons, "goodly physicians, Machaon and Podalirios," served with the Greek army at the destruction of Troy around 1200 B.C.[3] Strabo, the Greek geographer (63 B.C.?–?A.D. 24), also located Aesculapius's birth place in Thessaly, at Trikka, the site of the first temple built in Aesculapius's honor. In later times it was thought to be Epidauros, where the Aesculapian religion was centered in the most renowned and splendid of some two hundred temples for his worship throughout the Greek world.

The truth of the matter may well be that Aesculapius was a chieftain or prince of Thessaly who was trained in medicine. Whatever his origin and early history, Aesculapius and his wife Epione had two daughters, Hygieia and Panaceia.

HYGIEIA AND PANACEIA

The daughters of Aesculapius are with us today. Hygieia has survived in the word "hygiene"—the practice of cleanliness in the maintenance of health; Panaceia in the word "panacea"—a remedy for all ills and difficulties. As Dr. Kate Campbell Hurd-Mead, a recognized American authority on women in medicine, puts it: "Homer merely mentions the sons of Aesculapius as healing the battle wounds at Troy, but the daughters' names . . . have become household words for the prevention of sickness."[4]

The generally accepted accounts tell little of Panaceia and her activities, but Hygieia is more than a remembered name. The Greeks, who believed in the healing power of nature and the practice of hygiene, erected hundreds of statues to her. Many depict a beautiful maiden feeding a serpent from a saucer of food held in her hand. There are others in which she is not alone, a rare occurrence for a goddess. She is shown performing treatment under the direction of her father, or, carrying her own medical staff, taking a basket of herbs to patients. Sometimes she is tending children in swaddling clothes. A votive tablet from Smyrna, Turkey, depicts a woman baring her cancerous breast to Hygieia. Goddess or talented mortal (and it is reasonable to assume that she shared the latter status with her father Aesculapius, chieftain of Thessaly), it is generally agreed that she functioned as a practicing physician.

A different view has been offered by the American surgeon Walter Addison Jayne:

> The family of Asklepios and his descendants devoted themselves to healing, which they considered their special prerogative, creating shrines and serving in the temples of the hero-god. Sacrifice was offered to his wife Epione at Epidauros, while his daughters attended upon him, assisted in the ritual, and administered to the sick. Hygieia was not a healer but simply represented Health. She aided in receiving the suppliants and cared for the sacred serpents. Legends concerning her suggest that the early development of her divinity and worship were apart from the Asklepios cult. . . . Panakeia was a definite healer, being the personification of the all-healing power of herbs and representing the omnipotence of the god in his art.[5]

THE SNAKE AS A SYMBOL OF HEALING

It may be difficult to attach a therapeutic value to the serpent that beguiled the woman into eating the fruit of the tree, but Moses in the wilderness at the Lord's command put a brass serpent on a pole, and "if a serpent had bitten any man, when he beheld the serpent of brass, he lived" (Numbers 21:9). In Greek mythology the snake had magical powers associated with prophecy, dreams, and healing. The Greeks also believed that the gods appeared on earth in the guise of serpents and, along with the Egyptians, Cretans, and Hindus, venerated the snake as the companion of the gods.

In ancient times a species of harmless yellow snakes, now extinct, flourished in the region of Epidauros. These reptiles were quite tame. Trained to lick the affected parts of the sick, they were used to being handled. The sick, who fed them cakes, regarded it as a good omen when the snakes approached.

In 293 B.C. when a plague was raging in Rome, its citizens asked that a mission be sent from the Aesculapian temple at Epidauros. As its transport sailed up the Tiber, a sacred snake slid from the deck and swam ashore. So great was the popular belief in the healing power of the sacred snakes that a temple to Aesculapius was built upon the spot where the snake landed.

By all accounts the daughters of Aesculapius fed the sacred snakes, and Aesculapius himself was seldom depicted without a rod with a sacred snake entwined about it. As a matter of fact, snake-entwined staffs considerably predate Aesculapius. The caduceus, modern symbol of medicine, a rod entwined with two snakes, though often confused with the Aesculapian symbol, is associated with Mercury (Hermes to the Greeks), the messenger of the gods. The single-snake staff of Aesculapius rather than the caduceus (the staff of Mercury) is the true symbol of medicine.

It is thought that the caduceus originated as an Assyro-Babylonian symbol "representing a god some of whose functions were medical," and was carried over from the earlier civilization into that of Greece and Rome.[6]

In ancient Egypt, the single-snake motif appears to have symbolized the gift of life and sovereignty, and the intertwined serpent motif was for the most part associated with fertility.[7]

Schouten has suggested that the caduceus was not adopted as a medical symbol until the Renaissance, when pharmacists and chemists were interested in alchemy, a science closely associated with

Mercury, both the god and the planet, and with the metal named after him (Mercurius Philosophorum). Since in "the 16th and 17th centuries the domains of pharmacy, chemistry, and medicine were not yet strictly demarcated and overlapped to some extent," the caduceus, attributed to Mercury, came "to be regarded as a medico-pharmaceutical emblem."[8]

WOMEN OF THE ANCIENT WORLD

Records on the practice of medicine by women in ancient times are scant. The loss of manuscripts, the burning of libraries, the fact that what books and records were handed down had to be copied by scribe or monk—all have taken their toll. However, enough evidence has remained from literary and archaeological sources to draw acceptable conclusions.

In the Stone and Bronze Ages there were women surgeons in Sumeria, Egypt, and Greece who used flint chisels and stick drills to relieve headache. The ancient Aztecs (whose female deity of healing took the form of a serpent), other American Indians, the inhabitants of some of the islands of the Pacific, and African jungle tribes often employed women healers. The Chinese and Siamese were using women in their hospitals as surgeons and midwives before 1000 B.C.

In Egypt the first woman doctor is said to have practiced around 2730 B.C. Egyptian queens took an early lead in matters medical. From Mentuhetep (c. 2300 B.C.) through Hatsheput (c. 1500 B.C.) to Cleopatra (69–30 B.C.), women rulers were often students of medicine. The medical school at Heliopolis was attended by women as early as 1500 B.C. The wife of Moses, Zipporah (c. 1200 B.C.?), is said to have trained there. Evidence from the Bible (Exodus 4:25) that she "took a sharp stone, and cut off the foreskin of her son" has been offered as proof that she regularly circumcised babies.

Gynecology, the study and treatment, surgical or otherwise, of diseases peculiar to women, and obstetrics (or midwifery) were taught at the women's medical school at the Temple of Saïs, near the Rosetta Mouth of the Nile River. An inscription at Saïs reads: "I have come from the school of medicine at Heliopolis, and have studied at the woman's school at Saïs where the divine mothers have taught me how to cure disease." This, says Dr. Hurd-Mead, shows quite plainly that medical women were professors at Saïs and taught pupils from all over the ancient world.[9]

Helen of Troy is said to have studied medicine in Egypt under Polydamna, wife of a Greek named Thonis. Helen apparently learned the medical use of nepenthe, the drug the ancients used to dull pain and sorrow. "Sweet Helen" with "the face that launched a thousand ships"[10] used the potion to poison her enemies as well as to cure her friends.

In Greece midwifery appears to have been entirely in the hands of women. That women also practiced medicine can be deduced from the fact that, about 300 B.C., women doctors were accused of the crime of performing abortions and were generally barred from practice. Their activity evidently had not been restricted to lying-in rooms.

The ban was broken by Agnodice, a pupil of Herophilus of Chalcedon (c. 300 B.C.). Dressing as a man, Agnodice was a great favorite among women patients. Unmasked and required to stand for trial for practicing under false pretenses, she was stoutly defended by the women of Athens, who told the judges: "You are not our husbands but our enemies if you condemn our Agnodice, who saves lives."[11] Thereafter she was permitted to dress her hair and body as she chose.

Corinth fell to Rome in 146 B.C., and hundreds of Greek women were taken prisoner. The medical women among them brought the highest prices in the slave market in Rome.

In the later days of the Roman Empire women practitioners were on an equal footing with men. The legal description of doctors was *medicus, sive masculus, sive foemina.* Seneca (4 B.C.?–A.D. 65), Roman statesman and philosopher, praised the skillful fingers of his woman doctor. In the following centuries men wrote about gynecology and obstetrics while women did the work, which was not limited to childbirth and the diseases of women. The women assisted their physician fathers, husbands, and brothers in the full range of medical activity.

WOMEN IN THE EARLY CHRISTIAN ERA

As Christianity rose to power the status of women suffered a decline. The early Church stressed female inferiority. By A.D. 581 the Church Fathers were declaring that women, far from being reasoning animals, were brutes without souls. The education of women came almost to a standstill.[12] There were a few, however, who were undaunted and whose names have been recorded.

Among them was Saint Bridget (453–525), who managed to practice medicine and midwifery in Ireland. She must have exerted substantial influence, for she persuaded the rulers to banish quacks from the country.

Another was Saint Scholastica, sister of Saint Benedict (480–544), who accompanied him throughout Italy while plague was raging. They helped the sick and taught others how to do so. Later she "established hospitals and trained nurses . . . to bathe the sick, give them medicine and food, and pray with the dying."[13]

Saint Walpurga (d. 779?), an English princess, studied medicine and founded a monastery at Heidenheim in Germany. Pictures show her with a flask of urine in one hand and bandages in the other. Walpurgis Night, the eve of May Day when witches are supposed to ride to an appointed rendezvous, is so named because May Day is also the feast of Saint Walpurga.

Not until the end of the first millennium after the birth of Christ do noted women practitioners reappear in historical records.

2. Women Practitioners of the Middle Ages

TROTULA AND THE SALERNO SCHOOL

The medical school at Salerno in southern Italy was formally founded by Constantinus Africanus in 1075, but a practical school of medicine had already flourished there for at least a hundred years. The school was coeducational, had no religious bias, and included a number of women teachers.

The best-known woman on the faculty was Trotula. Her title was *magistra medicinae*. Rudolph (or Raoul) Malecouronne (or Mala-Corona), who was regarded as the most important eleventh-century physician in western France and who had studied at Salerno sometime between 1040 and 1059, reported that there was only one teacher there wise enough to meet him in argument and answer his questions, and that was a woman *(sapiens matrona)*. It seems certain that the wise woman to whom he was referring was Trotula.

She appeared under a variety of names in literature and in legend: Trotta, Trocta, Tortolo, Trocula, and many other combinations of some or all the letters in her name, as well as *Uxor Platearii* (wife of Platearius), *Mulier sapiens* (wise woman), Eros Juliae, and Erotian. Copies of her famous works on obstetrics and gynecology were made by scribes, who, as the years passed, became careless of the names of the authors whose works they copied. Her books as often as not carried the name of an early Christian writer—Eros or Erotian. This has led to some question as to whether Trotula really existed.

44

Dr. Hurd-Mead has thoroughly reviewed the manuscripts and printed editions of Trotula's writings in order to answer those historians who have doubted "the identity and even the actual existence of . . . the author of 'the *Trotula maior* and *minor.*' " She undertook to prove that Trotula "was a very real person of the eleventh century, a *magistra medicinae,* and not an ordinary midwife, or even a mythical person, as has been suggested; and that the book which was for centuries attributed to her was authentic, and not written by a man." From the evidence Dr. Hurd-Mead has concluded that it could be said "without fear of contradiction that, for nearly five hundred years after Trotula's death, her writings were highly prized, and had a wide distribution. From no source whatsoever up to this point does there appear to have been any doubt of her identity, or any question that she was the author of the works attributed to her."[1]

Another modern historian, Cecilia C. Mettler, agrees: "Trotula has been identified with various individuals, and it has been proposed that the name was merely a collective name for midwives in general. It is now conceded that Trotula had a separate existence."[2]

Not much is known about Trotula's personal life. She was the wife of John Platearius, and they had at least two sons, John and Matthew. Several of their descendants were surgeons. Together, husband and wife and son John compiled a medical encyclopedia known as the *Practica brevis.* John the younger also wrote a book on urine called *Regulae urinarum.*

More is known of her work. She was consulted by men and women. In the fields of obstetrics and gynecology she was far ahead of her time, and even performed caesarean sections. One of her cases was a woman patient who was referred to her for surgery with a diagnosis of hernia by another member of the faculty. Trotula diagnosed an abscess, lanced and drained it, and sent the patient home with medicated oils for healing purposes.

It is unlikely that Trotula ever dissected a human body. To have done so would have involved defying the laws of the Church. Conse-

quently her diagnoses had to be based largely on symptoms presented by the patient. According to Salvatore De Renzi, author of
a five-volume history of Italian medicine (1844–1848) and editor of
the Copenhagen Manuscripts of the School of Salerno, Trotula's
instructions to her students were practical:

> When you reach the patient ask where his pain is, then feel
> his pulse, touch his skin to see if it has fever, ask if he has had
> a chill, and when the pain began, and if it was worse at night,
> watch his facial expression, test the softness of his abdomen,
> ask if he passes urine freely, look carefully at the urine, exam-
> ine his body for sensitive spots, and if you find nothing ask
> what other doctors he has consulted and what was their diag-
> nosis, ask if he has ever had a similar attack, and when. Then,
> having found the cause of his trouble it will be easy to deter-
> mine the treatment.[3]

Trotula's great work was her book on gynecology. It is true that
much of her material came from a variety of earlier sources and that,
where it was original, it could not far exceed the general level of
medical knowledge in the eleventh century. But her book was so
practical a treatise on gynecology and midwifery that it became
regarded as the great authority for women doctors and midwives and
was copied and consulted for hundreds of years.

Trotula was not an M.D. The Doctor of Medicine degree was first
conferred in Salerno in 1180 but, it appears, only to men. A special
diploma was offered to women in the thirteenth and fourteenth
centuries. In 1430 the degree of Doctor of Medicine was awarded
to Constanza Calenda.

Among the medical women of Salerno there were several who did
not hesitate to write on scientific subjects that in later centuries
would be considered indelicate for women to study. The best of these
mulieres salernitanae, as they were called, were a Roman woman
named Abella; Mercuriada, a surgeon; and Rebecca of the Guarna

family, which numbered kings and princes of the Church among its members.

HILDEGARD OF BINGEN AND THE ABBESSES OF WESTERN EUROPE

There were no licensed doctors at the beginning of the twelfth century. The medical men of the day were mostly monks. In fact, a monk had only to copy a single medical manuscript to style himself *medicus*. Then, at the Council of Trent in 1125 and at the Lateran Council in 1139, the Church decreed that monks should neither let blood nor perform surgical operations. Bleeding, the treatment of wounds, and the setting of bones fell to women and barbers.

This was also the period which saw the growth of many religious retreats for women, and a number of abbesses played important roles in medicine. Héloise (1101–1164), best remembered for her love of Abélard, was probably the most learned medical woman in France. She was trained by Abélard, a physician as well as a philosopher. After his death in 1142 she devoted her life to teaching and practicing medicine at the Paraclete, a hermitage for women in Champagne.

Elizabeth of Schönau (1129–1165) founded a Benedictine nunnery near Trier in west Germany on the Moselle River near the Luxembourg border. Although she was named a *magistra medicinae* in 1157, she is less remembered for her medical skill and her kindness to the poor and the sick than for her prophecies and visions.

Herrade of Landsberg (d. 1195) was abbess of Hohenburg in Alsace. The abbey sat atop Mount Saint Odilia in the Vosges Mountains and was surrounded by castles and other religious houses. In 1187 Herrade built a large hospital on her convent grounds and became its physician-in-chief.

Other notable twelfth-century abbesses included Gertrude of Ro-

bersdorf, Gertrude Countess Palatine of Nivelle, and Lioba of Fulda.
The most famous of them all was Hildegard of Bingen (1098–1180)
in the German Rhine country.

Hildegard was born of noble parents at Bückelheim on the river
Nahe near Sponheim, southwest of Mainz. Destined early to be a
religious, she passed almost her entire life within the walls of Benedictine houses. At the age of eight she was sent to nearby Disiboden-
berg, to study with the abbess, her aunt Yutta. At thirty she succeeded her aunt.

Hildegard, from early childhood, was subject to curious day-
dreams; the English physician and historian Charles Singer (1876–
1945) quotes her as saying: "These visions which I saw I beheld
neither in sleep, nor in dream, nor in madness, nor with my carnal
eyes, nor with the ears of the flesh, nor in hidden places; but wakeful,
alert, with the eyes of the spirit and with the inward ears I perceived
them in open view and according to the will of God. And how this
was compassed is hard indeed for human flesh to search out."[4]

Dr. Lauder Brunton, a Victorian physician, believes that "Hildegard was a hysterical female and it is possible that her visions were
on this basis. However, they all show remarkable similarity and
depict the usual visual aura of migraine, that is, brilliant points on
a bright background with wavy fortification lines."[5]

But whether she suffered from migraine headaches, epileptic at-
tacks, muscular seizures, or hysteria, as various authorities have
suggested, or was a true visionary, her visions were very real to her.

Hildegard was not only gifted with an active mind and an efficient
intellect, but possessed great energy and considerable literary power.
Her wide-ranging writings reveal her varied activities and her remarkable faculty for imaginative flight. She is said to have written
fourteen works, some in several volumes—medical and psychologi-
cal treatises, works on religious instruction, accounts of her visions
and prophecies. She foretold the fall of the Holy Roman Empire, still
seven centuries away, and she predicted the reformation of the
Church that would take place four hundred years after her death,

indicating that it would be caused in part by the corruption of the clergy.

In her medical and scientific writings—which Dr. Hurd-Mead has described as "the most important Latin scientific contributions produced in Europe during the Middle Ages"[6]—Hildegard foreshadowed such later discoveries as the circulation of the blood, the causes of contagion and of autointoxication, nerve action originating in the brain, and the chemistry of the blood. She is credited with at least two medical treatises, the *Liber simplicis medicinae* and the *Liber compositae medicinae,* and a little tract on clinical medicine, *Causae et curae.* The *Liber simplicis* deals with herbs, plants, minerals, precious stones, and food substances. An eminent Pomeranian medical historian, Kurt Polycarp Joachim Sprengel (1766–1833), attributed to Hildegard the use of fern against all types of "deviltry," of herring in the treatment of itch, and of vetch for curing warts.[7]

In 1147 Hildegard and some of her nuns built a new convent at Rupertsberg in the hills above the River Nahe, across from the important medieval town of Bingen, where the Nahe joined the Rhine. The Rhine was the highway of western Germany, and Hildegard was well placed for observing its traffic and the activities of men. The basin of the Nahe and the Glan she knew intimately, and she traveled as far north as Cologne, as far east as Frankfurt am Main, and southeast to Rothenburg ob der Tauber. Her journeys were in the nature of religious progresses, but her efforts at stimulating spiritual revival were too often directed against the cruelly persecuted Cathari, a heretical Albigensian sect that spread across the Rhine country in the twelfth century. Her excessive religious ardor was counterbalanced by the fact that, on the same journeys, she taught medicine, theology, and gave advice to abbesses, prioresses, and nuns.

She traveled on horseback, accompanied by a troop of nuns and servants. In the crude, uncomfortable conditions of life in the twelfth century, this was quite an undertaking for any woman, and she continued to make these journeys until she approached eighty. Most of her contemporaries did not live to half that age.

What Hildegard could not accomplish in person she covered with her pen. She was in constant touch with Mayence, the seat of the archbishopric in which Bingen was situated, and she wrote extensively to churchmen in towns throughout Germany, the Low Countries, and Central Europe. Her correspondence with Saint Bernard of Clairvaux, then preaching his crusade, with four popes who filled the Holy See in the course of her long lifetime—Eugenius III, Anastasius IV, Adrian IV, and Alexander III—and with the emperors Conrad and Frederick Barbarossa brought her into the mainstream of European history. In her letters she practically "dictated to popes, emperors, and kings the courses of action they should take."[8] She even had contact with Henry II of England and his consort, Eleanor of Aquitaine, the divorced wife of Louis VII of France.

Hildegard died on September 17, 1180, at eighty-two. Though the title of "saint" was later accorded her, she was never in fact canonized. Attempts to achieve her elevation were made under Gregory IX (1237), Innocent IV (1243), and John XXII (1317), but all failed. As Dr. Singer has pointed out: "Miraculous cures and other works of wonder were claimed for her, but either they were insufficiently miraculous or insufficiently attested. Those who have impartially traced her life in her documents will agree with the verdict of the Church. Hers was a fiery, a prophetic, in many ways a singularly noble spirit, but she was not a saint in any intelligible sense of the word."[9]

The Thirteenth Century to the Renaissance

The years that followed the death of Hildegard of Bingen produced no women medical writers and practitioners of her stature, no teachers to rival Trotula. This does not mean that women were not actively engaged in medicine and surgery.

Some names that have come down to us would seem to indicate that royal women were once again active in furthering the cause of medicine. Many founded hospitals in which they also worked. Among them were Blanche of Castile, mother of Louis IX of France, and Beatrice of Savoy, his mother-in-law; Blanche's daughter, Marguerite of Bourgogne, queen of Sicily; two of Blanche's sisters, Urraca, queen of Portugal, and Berengaria, queen of Castile; Elizabeth of Aragon, who succeeded Urraca as queen of Portugal; Queen Hedwig of Polish Silesia and her daughter-in-law, Princess Anna of Bohemia.

In Italy, where the universities had never been closed to women, Salerno and Bologna steadily turned out women practitioners. The impetus for this may well have been the decree of Charles, duke of Calabria, that women be attended by women practitioners for all illness, not merely labor, thus creating a need for trained women surgeons.

James Walsh, an American physician and scholar of the 1920s, found that the anatomist Mondino de Luzzi (1270–1326) held his assistant Alessandra Giliani (1307–1326) of Perciceto in high regard. She "would cleanse most skilfully the smallest vein, the arteries, all ramifications of the vessels, without lacerating or dividing them, and to prepare them for demonstration she would fill them with various coloured liquids, which, after having been driven into the vessels, would harden without destroying the vessels. Again, she would paint these same vessels to their minute branches so perfectly, and colour them so naturally, that, added to the wonderful explanations and teachings of the master, they brought him great fame and credit."[10]

In 1390 Dorothea Bocchi succeeded her father as professor of medicine and moral philosophy at Bologna and taught there for forty years.

The religious continued their good works. Saint Catherine of Siena (d. 1380), the daughter of a tanner, devoted her life to the care of the sick, especially those with plague and other contagious diseases. In the 1400s the work of two other Italian medical women brought them sainthood. Catherine of Bologna (1413–1463), abbess of the nunnery of the Poor Clares, taught the sisters medicine so that they could prescribe for their patients as well as nurse them. Their instruction covered interpretation of urine and the pulse, the diagnosis of disease, and how to recognize the onset of death. In fatal cases they prayed with their patients. Catherine of Genoa, the youngest of five children in the noble Fieschi family, was known for her devotion to the sick. During the plague she unhesitatingly moved among the victims and treated them.

Any discussion of medical saints must include the Scandinavian Bridget (1304–1373), founder of the Brigittine order. She is probably best remembered for the Syon convent, established and endowed by Henry V in 1415, which became the best medical training school in England. Another woman working in England about the same time was Cecilia of Oxford, who was employed as court surgeon by Queen Philippa, wife of Edward III.

In the early 1400s Joan, widow of William of Lee who was killed during Henry IV's expedition against Owen Glendower of Wales, petitioned the king to be allowed to make her living by the practice of "physic"—that is, medicine: "May it please your highness and most gracious lordship to grant to the aforesaid poor bedeswoman a letter under your great seal, that she may safely go about the country to practice her art without hinderance and disturbance from all folk, who despise her by reason of her said art, In God's name and by way of charity."[11] Whether her request was ever granted is not known, but in 1421 the physicians of England petitioned Parliament, asking that no man be allowed to practice medicine unless he had a degree in physic from a university and that no woman be permitted to practice under any circumstances.

In France women practiced the general art of healing in addition to midwifery. Louis IX was accompanied on the Sixth Crusade (1248–54) by a female doctor. Toward the end of the thirteenth century a list of thirty-eight medical practitioners in Paris included the names of eight women.

In 1311 Philip the Fair issued an edict forbidding any surgeon, male or female *(aucun chirurgien ou aucune chirurgienne),* to practice in Paris unless he had been carefully examined and approved by the Sworn Master Surgeons. Seemingly this put men and women on the same footing. But in practice, it did not prevent discrimination against women in the granting of licenses. Between 1312 and 1327 the French prior of Sainte Geneviève excommunicated a number of women for practicing medicine without a license. One of them, Clarisse of Rotomago (or Rouen), defied the ban and continued to practice.

In 1322, Jacoba Felicie, a woman of good birth, was arraigned before the Court of Justice at Paris by the Dean and Masters of the Faculty of Medicine. The charge was practicing medicine in the city and suburbs, contrary to an ancient ordinance forbidding anyone to do so who had not studied and received the degree of Master of Medicine from the Faculty and been approved by the Chancellor. The charge read:

> That the said Jacoba visited many sick folk labouring under severe illness in Paris and the suburbs, examining their urine, touching, feeling and holding their pulse, body and limbs, (2) that after this examination she was wont to say to the said sick folk "I will cure you, by God's will, if you will trust me," making a compact with them and receiving money there from, (3) that after the said compact was made between the said party and the sick folk or their friends that she would cure them of their internal sickness or of wounds upon their outward body, the aforesaid party used to visit them several times assiduously and continually inspecting their urine and feeling and touching their limbs, (4) and that after this she gave and gives to the aforesaid folk sirups to drink, conformative, laxa-

tive and digestive, as well liquid as not liquid, and aromatic and other potions, which they often drink and have drunk in her presence and at her order, (5) and that she continues so to practice though unqualified in the schools of Paris and unlicensed by the Chancellor of Paris and the Dean of Magistrates, (6) that she has been warned and inhibited but (7) goes on as before.[12]

In an attempt to win their case, the prosecutors called eight men and women to testify that Jacoba had indeed employed the methods of diagnosis and treatment outlined in the charge, but the witnesses went on to say that she was regarded as a wise physician and had successfully cured them. In fact, a few added that they had previously been given up by doctors whose names they named, to the embarrassment of the profession as a whole and of the Faculty of Medicine in particular. All testified that Jacoba made no monetary arrangements ahead of time. Patients paid her what they thought appropriate after she had cured them.

What the doctors really were objecting to was her use of all the regular methods of diagnosis and treatment.

In her answering plea Jacoba argued that the statute under which she was charged was intended to restrain foolish persons ignorant of the art of medicine. She pleaded that she be judged by her results. Then she went on to speak of the general need for women doctors:

It is better and more seemly that a wise woman learned in the art should visit a sick woman and inquire into the secrets of her nature and her hidden parts, than that a man should do so, for whom it is not lawful to see and seek out the aforesaid parts, nor to feel with his hands the breasts, belly and feet, &c., of women; a man should ever avoid and flee as much as he can the secrets of women and of their societies. And a woman before now would allow herself to die rather than to reveal the secrets of her infirmity to a man, on account of the honour of the female sex and of the shame which she would feel. And for these reasons many women and also men have perished of their infirmities, not being willing to have doctors, lest these should see their secret parts. And concerning this there is and has been public knowledge and rumour and the Dean and Masters will not deny it.[13]

The reply filed by the prosecution ignored her case for women doctors and concentrated on Jacoba herself. They argued that, since she had not been approved by the Faculty, she must therefore be utterly ignorant of the art of medicine. As to her cures, they were "certain that a man approved in the aforesaid art could cure the sick better than such a woman." They also argued that, since women were barred from being advocates or witnesses in criminal cases, they should the more so be barred from practicing medicine, it being worse to kill a man than to lose a lawsuit.[14]

The outcome was a foregone conclusion. Jacoba Felicie was enjoined from practicing the healing profession. She was not, of course, alone in receiving such treatment at the hands of the Faculty of Medicine.

In 1352 the French king, John the Good, legalized the practice of medicine by specially qualified women, but the eminent surgeon, Gui de Chauliac (1300–1370) continued to favor the exclusion of women because of their sex. He finally conceded that properly trained women might be permitted to bleed, administer herbs, make elixirs, reduce fractures, and function as midwives.

In other parts of Europe women were also active. In 1394 fifteen women were licensed to practice medicine in Frankfurt am Main. Among them was a remarkable surgeon, the daughter of Hans der Wolff, who trained her. She was awarded several medals for treating the wounded. Marguerite of Naples, an eye specialist, became court physician to King Ladislaus in 1414. In 1406 the Holy Roman Emperor Sigismund appointed women on good salaries to treat the poor because male doctors refused to go to patients' homes or take care of them for nothing.

There were some Jewish women practitioners despite the generally tenuous position of the Jews in the Middle Ages. Jews were believed to have special knowledge and skills in medicine, abilities not confined to the males. It is known that around 1326 Sarah of Saint Gilles headed a large private medical school in the university town of Montpellier in southern France. A woman named Zerlin was in practice in Frankfurt. In 1419 Bishop Johann II granted another Sarah permission to practice at Würzburg. Jacoba was sometimes referred to as a "Jewess," and among her contemporaries brought to trial was a woman named Belota.

The full acceptance of women by the medical profession was far in the future. The arguments presented by Jacoba at her trial were still being advanced six hundred years later.

3. The Science of
Midwifery

It comes as somewhat of a surprise to find that in centuries past there were men midwives as well as women midwives. As a profession for men it was generally held in contempt. In many eras the people were as strongly set against male midwives as they would later be against women physicians. It was considered to be indecent for a woman and her newborn baby to be touched by a strange man. Not until the end of the nineteenth century did the male of the species become a recognized member of the medical profession, with his own specialty —obstetrics and gynecology.

From earliest times, however, men have written about the subject, and their efforts at raising the standards of midwifery have been of benefit to all.

Soranus of Ephesus (A.D. 98–138), in his book for women medical students of his day, set the criteria for an *obstetrix* (midwife). She must be able to read and write and must be free from superstitions. In addition to a keen intellect and good sight and hearing, she must have strong arms and legs, soft hands, long, thin fingers, and short, clean nails. She must be versed in anatomy, hygiene, and therapeutics, and must be able to distinguish between normal and abnormal conditions of the body. Finally, she must love her work and must keep secrets honorably. In short, that "midwife is the most capable who knows the whole realm of therapy, dietetics, surgery, pharmacy, and who can give good advice, is not worried by sudden complication and is prepared to save her patient's life if possible, for she will often be called to visit the seriously sick."[1]

The picture painted by Soranus was not to be fully realized until the sixteenth century, and his ideal midwife is a far cry from the midwife of today who is thought of as a woman who does little more than help other women in labor and childbirth. The sixteenth, seventeenth, and eighteenth centuries saw a succession of outstanding midwives.

LOUYSE BOURGEOIS

Louyse Bourgeois (1563–1636) was born in the aristocratic district of Saint-Germain, beyond the walls of Paris. The family laid no claim to membership in the nobility, though her father was evidently a man of substance. She was taught to read and write.

Louyse married at an early age. Her husband, Martin Boursier, had been a pupil of the great army surgeon and master midwife, Ambroise Paré (1510–1590), and continued to live in Paré's house as his assistant for twenty years. By some accounts, Louyse also studied under Paré. However, since Paré was close to seventy when Boursier married her, it seems more likely that she was trained by her husband. In any event Louyse clearly knew Paré, for she wrote in one of her books of seeing "the great surgeon Paré, lying on his death-bed, and, although at the age of eighty, with as unclouded an intellect as ever, and as anxious as ever to learn something from those who visited him."[2]

She was trained in the tradition of Paré, who has been described as having "created a new epoch in surgery and greatly advanced the science of midwifery." Just when Paré's interest in midwifery was aroused is uncertain, but it probably developed during the three years in the mid-1530s he spent as a resident at the Hôtel Dieu in Paris, "where the abominable practices of many of the midwives must have filled him with horror."[3]

Louyse, who seems to have had a natural aptitude for midwifery, gained experience practicing on the poor of the neighborhood in which she and her husband lived. This was fortunate, for during the political upheaval of 1588–89 that ended with the ascension of Henry IV to the throne, her husband found it impossible to earn a living. According to William Goodell, a nineteenth-century Philadelphia physician, Boursier "seems to have been a man of good parts and an affectionate husband, for his wife speaks very kindly of him, and expresses her great indebtedness to him for her knowledge of midwifery; but he was without snap. His family increased more rapidly than his practice, and the outlook was not good."[4]

No midwife might legally practice in Paris until she became a *matrone jurée* (sworn matron). Louyse had practiced among the poor for five years without this license. Now that she had to seek wealthier patients to support her family, she could no longer evade the law. Admission as a sworn matron to what amounted to a guild of midwives required the endorsement of one physician, two surgeons, and two midwives. The first three presented no difficulty. Not so the midwives, who wanted to know the nature of her husband's business. When they learned that he was a surgeon they said, first, that he should support her and, second, that his status would give her an unfair advantage over other midwives. "We must enroll the wives of tradesmen only, who will not injure our business."[5] Ultimately she obtained her license and her clientele was quickly extended, first to the gentry and then to the nobility.

Madame Boursier was thirty-six when she was called to attend Marie de' Medici, Henry IV's wife. It was the fashion at that time for courtiers to engage male midwives for their mistresses. The king, however, had come to rely on *la dame* Dupuis, who had safely delivered his mistress, *la belle* Gabrielle, four times. It was understandable that he would prefer a woman for his wife. His confidence was justified. Madame Boursier brought the queen through seven confinements. Of the birth of the future Louis XIII she wrote:

> The obstetrical chair was also brought in; it was covered with crimson velvet. About 4 o'clock in the morning a great colic, mingling itself among the travail of the queen, gave her terrible

pain without helping her along. From time to time the king
made one of the doctors come to see the queen and speak to
me so that I might know what was taking place. . . . The
doctors asked me, "If this were a woman and you were alone
with the case, what would you do?" I proposed to them some
remedies which they ordered at once from the apothecary,
who proposed to them others . . . which he said in similar cases
had done much good. Knowing the great zeal which the
apothecary had in the service of her majesty, and knowing that
if the remedy did not do all the good he claimed for it, it could
not do her any harm, I made no protest, so they gave it to her.[6]

Madame Boursier's day at court lasted for twenty-seven years.
Then in 1627 the Duchesse d'Orléans died of virulent puerperal
peritonitis while under her care. The report of an autopsy performed
by ten physicians was critical of her. She replied in print, and her
defense was so telling that none of the physicians dared openly to
pick up the challenge. But her career was over. She devoted her
remaining nine years to writing her memoirs.

Madame Boursier was the first midwife to publish a work on
obstetrics. This was in 1609. A second edition appeared in 1617 and
a third (considerably enlarged) in 1626. The sixth edition in 1634
included an appendix (a "collection of secrets") in which the medical
treatment of many diseases was outlined. New editions continued to
appear for over one hundred years. The practice of forcing labor
prematurely in cases involving severe hemorrhaging was one of her
innovations.

When a pregnant woman has too great a loss of blood, the
child must be manually extracted. The wife of a certain sena-
tor, six months pregnant, having shown these symptoms, I
delivered her by version [turning the baby], and not an hour
too soon. Her life was saved and the baby lived for two days.
. . . If I had known earlier that this would stop the hemorrhage,
I could have saved the life of the Duchess of Montbazon.[7]

In the 1609 work, which was dedicated to Marie de' Medici, she named no less than twelve positions in which the unborn baby might be found, and she laid down rules for the handling of each.

In the 1626 edition she added a chapter entitled "Advice to my Daughter"—the daughter was also a midwife—in which she described some of the situations with which she had had to contend. The midwife was required to stay with the patient for five weeks before the birth of the baby. At the critical time the family entered the room and walked up and down with the mother-to-be. The patient might be delivered standing, kneeling, on the bed, or on an obstetrical chair, which dated back in basic design to Hippocrates. She told how, after the birth of one of the royal princes, two hundred persons crowded into the room. When she had to resuscitate an apparently lifeless infant, she passed warm wine from her own mouth into the infant's mouth to cut the phlegm, and she rubbed the body vigorously and bathed it in warm wine and water.

For her services to the royal family Madame Boursier was paid one thousand ducats for the birth of a boy and six hundred for a girl. She received, in addition, many presents. The pension for life that the king had promised her never materialized, despite the fact that she had saved the lives of several royal babies.

A year before her death the midwives of Paris petitioned the Faculty of Medicine to have her conduct a public course in obstetrics, but the faculty members, preoccupied with quarrels among physicians, barbers, and surgeons, turned them down.

A notable private pupil of Madame Boursier was Marguérite du Tertre de La Marche (1638–1706). For many years she was in charge of the midwives at the Hôtel Dieu, where she established a three-month course of training. She taught them, among other things, how to handle their cases without the help of a surgeon. In 1677 she published a book of instructions for midwives, which revealed that she was a master of the art as well as an outstanding teacher.

ENGLISH MIDWIVES

In seventeenth-century England great improvements in midwifery were made, for which both men and women midwives were responsible. Percival Willughby (1596–1685) kept records of his cases and published some of them under the title *Observations in Midwifery.* His purpose was to improve the skill of country midwives, for the most part women who received no proper training, "to inform [them] with such ways as [he had] used with great successe."[8]

He didn't limit his teaching to the management of natural birth. Abnormal labor was a common occurrence, usually caused by "the infirmity called rickets." Untrained midwives met this condition by resorting to the use of "pothooks, pack-needles, silver spoons, thatcher's hooks and knives, to show their imagined skils." To prevent such barbarities, he carefully trained his students in what he called the "Handy Operation."[9] He was aware of the need for a truly scientific instrument and may have heard rumors of the obstetrical forceps, which was invented by the Chamberlens, a family of male midwives. The Chamberlens, however, did not make their instrument public until thirty years after Willughby's death.

Willughby taught midwifery to one of his two daughters, and she appears to have been highly successful in the art, assisting her father in difficult cases. Most often, because of strong prejudice against male practitioners, Miss Willughby was the midwife of record.

The prejudice was fanned by the women midwives, who often crossed verbal swords with their male counterparts. In 1634, when Peter Chamberlen III (1601–1683) attempted to establish a Corporation of Midwives with himself as governor, the female midwives resisted. Either misunderstanding his motives or fearing the power he might assume, they accused him of interfering with their business. This was a pity. The Chamberlens sincerely believed that London midwives should be far better trained and educated, and it was part of their proposed program to institute such teaching. This was the second attempt by the Chamberlens to organize the midwives. An earlier petition by Peter the Elder (1560–1631) and Peter the Younger (1572–1626) to Sir Francis Bacon, a member of the Privy Council, for the incorporation of a Society of Midwives had been rejected on the grounds that self-government for midwives was "neither necessary nor convenient."[10]

The best-known women midwives of the period were Jane Sharp and Mrs. Elizabeth Cellier.

Jane Sharp, after she had been in practice for thirty years, published *The Compleat Midwife's Companion* in 1671. She hoped that her book would assure the common people as safe and rapid deliveries as the delicate ladies of the nobility. She was clearly prejudiced against males as fellow workers, for she advised the midwives of England to place greater reliance on God than in the College of Physicians.

Elizabeth Cellier's reputation as a midwife was excellent. She was well educated and financially secure. Unwilling to leave things as they were, she battled in the cause of midwifery. She believed that professional status would only be achieved when the women midwives organized themselves for study and for work.

Outspoken Mrs. Cellier was condemned to stand in the pillory on more than one occasion. On April 30, 1680, she was arraigned before Lord Chief Justice Scroggs for high treason, the charge being that "Elizabeth Cellier and other false traitors at the parish of St Clements Danes advisedly, devilishly, maliciously, and traitorously assembled, united, and gathered themselves together, and then and there devilishly, advisedly, maliciously, cunningly, and traitorously consulted and agreed to bring the said Lord the King to death and final destruction, and to depose and deprive him of his crown and government, and so introduce and establish the Romish religion in this kingdom."[11]

The jury returned a verdict of not guilty and, as was customary, applied to Mrs. Cellier for a guinea apiece. She wrote to the foreman declining to pay but making this offer instead: "Pray, Sir, accept of and give my most humble service to yourself and all the worthy gentlemen of your pannel, and yours and their several ladies; and if you and they please, I will with no less fidelity serve them in their deliveries than you have done me with justice in mine."[12]

She compiled statistics showing that, in the twenty years from 1642 to 1662, 6000 English women died in childbirth, 5000 babies were born dead, and 13,000 were aborted. She claimed that two-thirds of these losses were attributable to lack of skill on the part of women practicing midwifery.

She laid plans for a royal hospital, to be well staffed and a model of neatness. Her plans even included a program for raising the money that would be needed. In June 1687 she presented to King James II a "scheme for the foundation of a Royal hospital and raising a revenue of five or six thousand pounds a year, by and for the maintenance of a corporation of skilful midwives, and such foundlings or exposed children as shall be admitted therein."[13] The king agreed to proceed in the matter and then quietly forgot all about it.

Elizabeth Cellier was no less vehement when the king failed to keep his promise than she had been on other occasions. This time she not only wound up in the pillory but was forced to witness the burning of her books, an extremely severe punishment in days when a library was a luxury.

There were other notable midwives in England. Hester Shawe (flourished 1634) of Barking Parish, London, was paid almost one thousand pounds for her skill by Abraham Perrot, Gentleman, in August 1666.

On June 10, 1687, a Mrs. Labany delivered Mary of Modena, queen to James II, of James Francis Edward, afterward called the Pretender. It was held by many that the prince was stillborn and that Mrs. Labany smuggled in and substituted a strange baby. Hugh Chamberlen, who would have been on the case had he not been detained by a patient in Chatham, declared the suggestion absurd.

Despite this rumor, "she received from the King, at the hands of Sidney Lord Godolphin, the enormous fee of 500 guineas—a sum more than sufficient to recompense her for her skill and compensate her for any pecuniary losses she may have sustained through her character being misrepresented."[14]

JUSTINE DITTRICHIN SIEGEMUNDIN

Midwifery developed more slowly in Germany than in France and England. The seventeenth century did, however, produce a most distinguished midwife in Justine Dittrichin Siegemundin (1650–1705).

Justine's father, a pastor in Rohnstock, Silesia, died when she was four and she received little education. At seventeen she married a master of horse. Two years later, believing herself to be pregnant, she sent for a midwife, who declared that she was in labor. But nothing happened. Three more midwives confirmed the diagnosis of the first. Finally a soldier's wife examined her and found not only that she was not in labor but that she was not even pregnant. This experience prompted Justine to learn all she could about the physical form and function of her sex. She read two treatises on male and female sex organs written by Reinier de Graaf (1641–1673) of Delft, Holland, which greatly influenced her decision to become a truly scientific midwife.

For twelve years she practiced among the local poor and taught other midwives, who frequently called her in as a consultant. As her fame spread she was employed by the upper-class women of Liegnitz, in what is now Poland. In due course she was appointed court midwife to the Electorate of Brandenburg and midwife to the royal family of Prussia. In 1688 she was called to Berlin to attend the wife of Frederick I (1657–1713) of Prussia.

A year later she published at her own expense a volume on midwifery generously illustrated with copperplate engravings. Many of the illustrations were sketches she made of her own cases. She wrote

in German rather than the customary Latin so she would be understood (as Paré, a century earlier, had written his book in simple
French for those barber-surgeons who could not read Latin). Frau
Siegemundin was severely criticized, but the book was republished
six times and translated into Dutch.

Frau Siegemundin advocated giving nature an opportunity to
terminate labor without interference. She advised midwives to study
how to turn badly presenting babies so that minimum damage might
be done to the mothers during birth. Her instruments for this procedure were rudimentary—a noose or sling around a foot in order to
bring the feet down, sometimes a blunt hook. She also used the
practice of puncturing the amniotic sac (the so-called bag of waters)
to stop hemorrhaging, a procedure introduced at about the same
time by her French contemporary François Mauriceau (1637–1709),
whose book on the diseases of pregnancy (1668) was the recognized
authority until it was succeeded by the works of Madame Boivin,
published between 1812 and 1833.

French Midwives of
the Eighteenth Century

Angélique Marguérite le Boursier du Coudray (1712–1789) was
born at Clermont-Ferrand in the Auvergne. She studied at the Hôtel
Dieu in Paris and was licensed to practice in 1740. Shortly thereafter
she became the hospital's head midwife. Her methods of teaching
were unique. Though credit for the innovation is sometimes given
to the Englishman William Smellie (1697–1763), she seems to have
preceded him in using a manikin of a female torso so constructed
as to provide her pupils with practice in delivery.

In 1759 she was appointed by royal commission to visit obstetrical
hospitals in the French provinces and deliver lectures. Her salary of
three thousand livres a year was continued as a pension when she

retired. Her book on midwifery, published in 1759, went through five editions.

Madame Marie-Jonet Dugès (1730–1797) was first taught obstetrics by her midwife-mother and then by her husband, Louis Dugès, a health officer in Paris. Madame Dugès served as medico-legal midwife in the law courts and prison at Châtelet near Charleroi in Belgium. In 1775 she was appointed midwife-in-chief at the Hôtel Dieu in Paris, where she thoroughly reorganized the maternity department.

Marie-Louise Lachapelle (1769–1821), daughter of Madame Dugès, continued her mother's work. As a child she was her mother's constant companion and proved an apt pupil. At the age of fifteen, she handled an extremely difficult delivery, saving both mother and child. Widowed at the age of twenty-six, with a daughter to support, she turned seriously to the practice of midwifery.

In 1797 she succeeded her mother as midwife-in-chief at the Hôtel Dieu. Later, when the lying-in hospital was organized, she was appointed *sage-femme-en-chef,* working under Jean-Louis Baudelocque (1746–1810), its first instructor in midwifery and Paris's leading obstetrician. Baudelocque, who had himself been a pupil of midwives, envied Madame Lachapelle her supple hands. He admired her mental capacities and considered her the most remarkable midwife of her time in the handling of difficult cases.

Madame Lachapelle took time out to study in Heidelberg, Germany's oldest university. On her return to Paris she was asked to organize a maternity and children's hospital at Port Royal, southwest of Versailles.

During her lifetime Madame Lachapelle collected enough material for a three-volume *Pratique des Accouchements ou Mémoires et Observations Choisies.* The work was edited and published by her nephew Antoine Dugès (1787–1838), professor in the Faculty of Medicine at Montpellier, four years after she had died from cancer of the stomach.

Her material was based on forty thousand cases on which she had compiled statistics. She believed that instruments should be used as sparingly as possible (and never solely for the shortening of labor). She reported that she herself had interfered with nature in less than 2 percent of her cases. Her plea for the exclusion of all unnecessary persons from the lying-in room met with scant success, but some of her innovations for the management of labor fared better.

The treatise, which covered all aspects of midwifery, must have been too much for the typical midwife, especially since it lacked illustrations. It has, in fact, been described as "a monument by a devoted nephew to his accomplished aunt."[15]

Nonetheless Madame Dugès Lachapelle played a leading role in effecting many of the changes in favor of the pregnant woman and the newborn child that surfaced toward the end of the eighteenth century.

Marie Anne Victoire Gillain (1773–1847), who has been rated by some as the most outstanding obstetrician of her time, was born in the Paris suburb of Montreuil. She was educated by nuns at a hospital at Etampes, thirty miles south of Paris. At twenty-four she married Louis Boivin, an assistant at the Bureau of National Domains. Soon widowed, with one daughter, she studied midwifery and received her diploma in 1800. She settled in Versailles but, when her little daughter was killed in an accident, she returned to Paris, where she worked for eleven years under Madame Lachapelle. A break between them was caused by some petty jealousy—not, as has sometimes been stated, by the publication of her first book on midwifery, which did not appear until afterward. Refusing several attractive offers, Madame Boivin accepted a position at a servant's pay in a hospital for prostitutes. When she retired after thirty-five years of service, her pension was so small that she died a year later of paralysis and want.

This bare outline does not reveal the stature of this woman. She published a number of books between 1812 and 1833. Her final work had forty-one plates and one hundred and sixteen figures, all colored by herself. The book has been described by Hunter Robb, the late nineteenth-century medical writer, as being as modern as it could possibly be before the advent of bacteriology.[16]

Guillaume Dupuytren, the best-trained surgeon of his day, placed his only daughter in Madame Boivin's hands for a confinement that promised to be difficult, saying that she had an eye at the tip of each finger.

In 1827 the University of Marburg, Germany, conferred on Madame Boivin an honorary M.D.—*Doctor Honoris Causa,* an honor rarely extended to women.

Charles D. Meigs of Jefferson Medical College of Philadelphia, author of *Females and their Diseases* (1849), said of Madame Boivin: "Her writings prove her to have been a most learned physician, and as she enjoyed a very large practice, her science and her great clinical experience, as well as her own personal knowledge, are more to be relied on than that of all male physicians together."[17]

THE SIEBOLDS, MOTHER AND DAUGHTER

Regina von Siebold, wife of a physician at the court of Darmstadt, Germany, and her daughter Charlotte von Siebold (1761–1859) both received the title of doctor of obstetrics, (*i.e.,* midwife) from the University of Giessen. The mother had earlier earned her *sage femme* diploma from the school of midwives at Würzburg, and her Giessen degree (1815) was honorary. Charlotte, who had studied in Göttingen in 1811 and 1812, graduated from Giessen in 1817 and taught there.

In the year of Charlotte von Siebold's graduation, Princess Charlotte of England and her child were both lost in childbirth. Two years later Charlotte von Siebold was called to England to deliver the Duchess of Kent of the future Queen Victoria. Had as competent a midwife attended Princess Charlotte, Victoria might never have reigned.

Of these and other midwives of the eighteenth and early nineteenth centuries Dr. Hurd-Mead quotes Hunter Robb: "They should not be judged from the standpoint of the degenerated midwife of today. Their work was exceedingly important and their experience has been scarcely equalled since their day. . . . Such midwives were in many ways superior to the average obstetrician even of today; . . . [their] careful observation, conservatism in practice and sound common sense . . . are as necessary now as they were in the eighteenth century."[18]

The "degenerated midwifery of today" that Robb described in 1891 was largely responsible for the fact that in the early twentieth century midwives practically disappeared in the more advanced countries of the world. But in the 1970s, with a shortage of professional obstetricians, training in midwifery is again being encouraged, and midwives are reappearing as highly trained paramedical personnel.

PART TWO

The Struggle
for Women's Rights
in Medicine

4. Dr. Barry

The difficulties facing the nineteenth-century woman determined to get a medical education and achieve professional status and the lengths to which she might be forced to go are only too well illustrated by the case of Dr. James Barry (1797?–1865).

When Dr. Barry died, an autopsy revealed that "he" was not only a woman but also the mother of at least one child. Her masquerade, lasting more than half a century, is hard to credit. She must have been a consummate actress, for "Dr. James" not only served as Inspector-General of the British Army from 1856 to 1865 but also became the ranking medical officer in the army.

The history of James Barry (her real name is not known) prior to the day in 1812 on which she emerged, diploma in hand, from the University of Edinburgh is shrouded in mystery. As Dr. Alfred Swaine Taylor put it: "When, where, and how [Barry] passed through his medical studies no one knows, but he contrived to obtain a diploma as Doctor of Medicine from Edinburgh when only fifteen years of age."[1]

Still, this woman doctor had to have a birth and upbringing, and once Dr. Barry's sex was posthumously revealed the rumor mills ground exceedingly fast. The most popular account established her as the illegitimate daughter of the Prince Regent and a well-known Scottish lady. This was in line with the reputation of the future King George IV. The guilt-ridden mother, recognizing that this unprotected female would have to make her way in a man's world, is said to have provided her with every masculine advantage. This involved not merely attire and general education but also careful preparation for medical school. Dr. Lovejoy rounds out this picture by suggesting that Dr. Barry may have "belonged to that virginal type of woman, well represented in the medical profession, to whom the normal relationships of life are repugnant, and who *escapes* into various fields of service."[2]

Whatever her background and motivation, Dr. Barry seems to have been accepted for what she represented herself to be. The English general George Thomas, Earl of Albemarle, described her as she appeared to him in 1819 in these words: "There was at that time at the Cape [of Good Hope] a person whose eccentricities attracted universal attention—Dr. James Barry, staff-surgeon to the garrison and the Governor's medical adviser. Lord Charles [Somerset] described him to me as the most skilful of physicians, and the most wayward of men. . . . I shortly afterwards sat next to him at dinner at one of the regimental messes. . . . His style of conversation was greatly superior to that one usually heard at a mess-table in those days of *non*-competitive examination."[3]

Dr. Barry's advancement in the army was spectacular. "In fact," says Dr. Brunton, "her advancement was similar to that of the kangeroo, and on occasion she was promoted two steps at a time."[4] By 1827 she had risen to the rank of surgeon-major.

Wearing a sword and wielding a scalpel, Dr. Barry turned up in many quarters of the globe. Her operating techniques were expert and drew the plaudits of her peers. While she never seems to have been awarded a medal or honor of any sort, her bravery, especially at the battles of Waterloo and Balaclava, was a matter of record. She saw service in Europe, South Africa, Canada, Jamaica, and India, and may well have been in Scutari (Turkey) in 1854, at the same time as Florence Nightingale.

To elude the penetrating gaze of an army in the field was an extraordinary feat. Dr. Barry spent over fifty years as a member of an elite army officer corps without her secret's being penetrated, despite her short stature, slight build, and somewhat squeaky voice, which invited ribbing from fellow officers. Dr. Barry, however, had trained herself to be an excellent shot. Anyone who referred disparagingly to her beardless chin, the tone of her voice, her exclusiveness and fastidiousness, or her refusal of alcohol in any form ran the risk of being called out for a duel—with pistols. On one recorded occasion she so resented the teasing of an officer that she challenged him to a duel and shot him through the lungs. Later Dr. Barry herself was wounded in a duel.

She had a quick temper that led to a number of disputes, and she was frequently held to be insubordinate. On several occasions she was sent home under arrest to face court-martial proceedings, but she was returned to duty unpunished. In fact, it was not unusual for her to pick up a promotion en route. This preferential treatment becomes more understandable when it is realized that no one ever questioned her courage, her devotion to duty, or her skill as a doctor.

Dr. Barry refused medical attention during her last illness. When postmortem examination revealed she was a woman, the officials at the War Office and the ultra-conservative leadership of the British Medical Association huffed and puffed. They could not blow away the reality; it was useless to protest that she must have been a man —that army records said so, that her hair was short, that she wore trousers. Since there was no point to stirring up the ashes of the dead, authority simply decreed Dr. Barry a man. It was so stated in the death certificate. It was also implied on her gravestone at Kensal Green, London.

Some people maintained that these men at the War Office had known her secret all along and that this was why she was accorded preferential treatment. In any event, all of her records have mysteriously disappeared.

5. The First Steps: Dr. Hunt, Dr. Folger, Dr. Clarke

It was in the United States that the modern movement for the admisson of women to the medical profession had its beginning. Its ultimate success is frequently and properly attributed to the efforts of such respected pioneers as the Blackwell sisters, Marie Zakrzewska, Mary Putnam Jacobi, and Emily Dunning Barringer, but there were women before them who paved the way.

From the time of the landing at Plymouth Rock women as well as men practiced medicine in New England. This was to be expected. In colonial days women worked side by side with men in the fields and in the shops. Wives and mothers frequently shouldered the responsibility for family medical care.

In those days there were no medical schools. Many doctors were self-educated. Young men became doctors after an apprenticeship with a practicing physican. No such opportunity existed for women. Their medical services remained on a subprofessional basis until certain physicians, especially among the Quakers, undertook to teach them. Unfortunately the names of only a few of the early women doctors have been preserved.

The earliest female practitioner whose name has survived was a "Dr." Millikin of Mount Desert, Maine. In Maryland in the early seventeenth century, Katherine Hebden, the wife of Thomas who sold drugs and coffins, seems to have practiced both pharmacy and medicine. The records show that she received nineteen hundred pounds of tobacco from a Richard Lawrence in exchange for medical service, and that she "did chirugery upon the legg of Dr. John Greenwell . . . and did diet him for seven weeks or thereabouts."[1]

Mrs. Frances Combes (or Coomes), an apprentice of Kentucky's first doctor, George Hartt, practiced as early as 1780. She has been described as "a woman of vigorous intellect, great originality, fertility of resources, and strength of character, and her fame as a surgeon, physician and obstetrician extended beyond the limits of her state."[2]

Dr. Mary Lavinder (1776–1845) set up a practice of midwifery and pediatrics in Savannah, Georgia, in 1814. Shortly thereafter the city was decimated by a yellow-fever epidemic, a great fire, and a tropical storm. Dr. Lavinder established a visiting service to the poor and served as nurse and doctor. She was highly respected by local physicians. Her unfailing service to the community was memorialized in her obituary: "Every day of the year, her old-fashioned 'chair' with its well-known white horse (almost as old as his mistress) might be seen wending the way along the bylanes of the city, loaded with coffee, and sugar, tea, and 'grits,' and sometimes even with mattresses and blankets for the sick poor. She ministered to them as doctor, nurse, housekeeper, almoner, and lastly comforter. . . ."[3]

Dr. Sarah E. Adams (1779–1846) of South Carolina studied medicine under Dr. Milton Anthony, founder of the Medical College of Georgia, and established a practice in Augusta about a hundred years before the Georgia Medical Society admitted its first woman member.

HARRIOT K. HUNT

When American medical schools were established they followed the general European pattern, which barred women from seeking a medical degree. Because of this a number of women set up practice without benefit of degree, the sole qualification for so establishing themselves being practical experience. Many of these practices flourished, but this did not make their operators less anxious for or less ready to battle for a proper medical education.

Among the women who practiced medicine without a diploma was Harriot K. Hunt (1805–1875), who established herself in Boston in 1835 and quickly developed a large following. Her contribution to the feminist cause in medicine was the militancy with which, from 1847, she fought for admission of women to medical school. Her attempts were of no avail until 1850, when the dean of Harvard Medical School, Oliver Wendell Holmes (father of the famous jurist), submitted her application for admission to the medical faculty. According to Dr. Lovejoy, the faculty found that nothing in the statutes denied women the right to attend medical lectures. Dr. Hunt, the members said, might attend lectures, but they remained uncommitted in respect to a degree.[4] The students countered with resolutions that forced Dr. Hunt to withdraw:

> *Resolved*, That no woman of true delicacy would be willing in the presence of men to listen to the discussions of the subjects that necessarily come under consideration of the student of medicine.
>
> *Resolved*, That we object to having the company of any female forced upon us, who is disposed to unsex herself, and to sacrifice her modesty by appearing with men in the lecture room.[5]

Another writer, Dr. Carol Lopate, offers a slightly different account of what took place: "Harvard itself had tried to become coeducational in 1850 when, under Oliver Wendell Holmes, it accepted one woman and three Negro students. In reaction to this burst of liberalism, the students rioted. Although the main protest was against admitting the Negro students, the woman—Miss Harriet Hunt—had to withdraw her application as well."[6]

The resolutions, which make no mention of Negroes, would seem to support Dr. Lovejoy over Dr. Lopate.

LYDIA FOLGER FOWLER

About the same time that Harriot Hunt was attempting to get into Harvard, Lydia Folger Fowler (1822–1879) was trying to find a school in New York. Their backgrounds were quite different.

Lydia Folger was born on Nantucket, an island off the coast of Massachusetts. Her family can be traced to John Folger, who had reached America in 1635 at the age of seventeen. (John Folger was, incidentally, Benjamin Franklin's maternal grandfather.) Most of the Folgers were teachers, thinkers, and scientists. Consequently Lydia was assured of an education not generally available to women.

Lydia married when she was twenty-two. Her husband, Lorenzo Niles Fowler, was an ardent believer in phrenology, the pseudo science that claims that mental faculties and character can be deduced from the protuberances of the skull. Lydia quickly became involved and was soon lecturing to groups of women, not only on phrenology but also on anatomy, physiology, and hygiene. She wrote elementary books on these and related subjects—among them, *Familiar Lessons in Astronomy* (1847) and *Familar Lessons in Physiology* (1848). Close contact with the scientific and the pseudoscientific turned her thoughts in the direction of medicine. But where could she go for training and a degree in medicine? Elizabeth Blackwell, as we shall see, had by a fluke been admitted to Geneva College, New York, in November 1847 and had graduated in January 1849, but by and large regular medical institutions refused to admit women.

This was the period when women were just beginning to fight for their rights. At their first convention, held in Seneca Falls, New York, in 1848, they set forth eighteen grievances in "A Declaration of Sentiments," modeled on the Declaration of Independence. This attack, signed by one hundred "radicals," received plenty of publicity, most of it bad. But two groups of nonconformist medical men, one in Rochester and the other in Syracuse who were organizing a new medical school, the Central Medical College of New York at

Syracuse, decided to adopt a policy of coeducation. When it opened on November 5, 1849, Lydia Folger Fowler was one of three women in an enrollment of ninety-two students.

The college was notorious for advocating medical doctrines generally unacceptable to regular medical men, such as eclecticism and homeopathy. Eclecticism involved selecting what seemed to be the best features from each of the competing medical systems and stressed the use of plant remedies. Homeopathy, based on the assumption that "like cures like," claimed that drugs producing certain definable symptoms in healthy persons would cure illnesses that showed the same symptoms, provided such drugs were given in infinitely small doses.

The Central Medical College of New York did not long survive. The founding fathers were soon disagreeing as to its objectives and how it should be operated. Within a year it was split into the Rochester Eclectic Medical College (which closed in 1852) and the Syracuse Medical College, Eclectic (which survived until 1855). But the college continued long enough to confer an M.D. degree on Lydia Folger Fowler in 1850.

A year later Dr. Fowler was appointed professor of midwifery and diseases of women and children at the Rochester college. She thus became the first woman to hold a professorship in a legally authorized medical school in the United States. In the summer of 1851 she addressed the New York State Eclectic Medical Society; again, the first time any woman appeared before an organized society of medical men.

After the Rochester college closed its doors in 1852, Dr. Fowler practiced in New York City for eleven years, at the same time lecturing to classes of women at the Metropolitan Medical College, Eclectic. She was highly regarded as a doctor, a lecturer, and a medico-social writer, and doubtless would have had a satisfactory career if her husband had not decided to move his practice of phrenology to London. The move was a wise one for him. Queen Victoria and Prince Albert had set their seal of approval on the science of phrenology by having their children's heads read. But for Lydia Fowler the move spelled oblivion, for she never seems to have established herself there. She died in London of pneumonia at the age of fifty-seven.

NANCY TALBOT CLARKE

In the late 1840s Massachusetts passed a law requiring that physiology be taught in all public schools in the state. This presented a problem to women who wished to teach girls, for few of them had the necessary training. Nancy Talbot Clarke (1825–1901), young widow of a dentist, determined to qualify herself.

Physiology was taught in the medical schools, but none would accept women students. She decided to try anyway. Through relatives, Nancy made application for admission to the Cleveland Medical College. The school had been set up in the early 1830s as the medical department of Western Reserve College but existed in name only until November 1843. Possibly as a result of Mrs. Clarke's application, a faculty meeting on February 12, 1850, moved that "respectable ladies be admitted to the lectures on the same terms as gentlemen." However, when another motion was entered proposing that "respectable Negroes" be included, neither was acted upon.[7] Nevertheless, without further recorded faculty action, Mrs. Clarke was enrolled for the 1850–51 session.

A day after the session began on November 5, 1851, the faculty reversed itself, unanimously adopting a resolution stating that it was "inexpedient to admit female students to the lectures."[8] This resolution was not applied to Mrs. Clarke, who continued on to graduation in March 1852.

Dr. Clarke had by now given up the idea of teaching and went into practice in Boston in 1852. The following year she applied for membership in the Massachusetts Medical Society. The few other women doctors in the area did not have her advantage of a medical degree from a regular school. The distinction might not impress patients, but she saw in it a potential wedge to force the doors of the all-male medical societies.

Seemingly she was qualified. The by-laws of the Massachusetts Medical Society made no mention of sex. (There had been no medical women to take into account when these were drawn.) However, certain provisions had been included for the stated purpose of preventing injustice to "medical men." The society, relying on this fact, instructed its affiliated county societies, through which an applicant had to proceed, to examine male candidates only.

Nancy Talbot Clarke won the fight for a medical education but lost the one for equal status.

6. Elizabeth Blackwell

In October 1847 Dr. Charles A. Lee, dean of the faculty of the Geneva College of Medicine in upstate New York, received a letter from a Dr. Joseph Warrington of Philadelphia. Dr. Warrington wrote of a young lady, Elizabeth Blackwell, who had been studying privately in his office. Miss Blackwell had applied to a majority of the medical schools in the nation for admission and had been turned down. Dr. Warrington suggested that "since Geneva was in the country it might somehow be freer from prejudice than the big city schools and might consider enrolling a woman student."[1]

Dean Lee, an elderly, nervous, courtly gentleman, carried his problem to the college president, Benjamin Hale, who was opposed to the suggestion but did not wish to refuse Dr. Warrington directly. Dr. Warrington was a Quaker, and Quakers, Dr. Hale pointed out to Dr. Lee, expected others to share their enlightened views. But he saw a way out. The students were mostly country boys from neighboring farm villages, good-natured but given to rowdyism. They would never tolerate a female in their midst. The thing to do was to let them decide—and then inform Dr. Warrington (regretfully) of their decision.

Dr. Lee presented the proposal to the student body. He pointed out that a decision to admit must be unanimous and asked for an early vote. He was almost as confident of the outcome as Dr. Hale had been. But they reckoned without the frame of mind of these sons of farmers, tradesmen, and mechanics, who had beem studying hard for many weeks with little relaxation. The proposal carried sufficient prospect of excitement to interest them. Speech after speech—some serious, some satirical, some plain funny—carried their deliberations into the evening. The result was a unanimous decision that Miss Elizabeth Blackwell should be admitted as a fellow student.

The dean was dumfounded. It had not occurred to him that the student body might view the advent of a female student as a pleasant diversion. Nor did any such thought occur to Elizabeth Blackwell, when she received a copy of its welcoming resolution, which read:

> *Resolved*—That one of the radical principles of a Republican Government is the universal education of both sexes; that to every branch of scientific education the door should be equally open to all; that the application of Elizabeth Blackwell to become a member of our class meets our entire approbation; and in extending our unanimous invitation we pledge ourselves that no conduct of ours shall cause her to regret her attendance at this institution.[2]

EARLY DAYS

Elizabeth Blackwell (1821–1910) was born in Bristol, England, the daughter of Samuel Blackwell. Mr. Blackwell was not merely not a member of the Church of England, he was an outspoken dissenter.

In the 1830s the only good schools were run by the Church of England, and the children of dissenters were excluded from them. Mr. Blackwell wanted his children, boys and girls alike, to enjoy a thorough education, and this was being achieved through the employment of tutors. But like many of his persuasion Mr. Blackwell looked yearningly toward the New World, with its freedom of thought and other democratic ideals. In 1832 fire destroyed Mr. Blackwell's sugar refinery in Bristol. This offered the opportunity he had been waiting for. He decided to build his new plant in America.

In their new country the Blackwells found friends among the

people who thought as they did about the problems of the day—abolitionists and leaders of the women's rights movement. In 1838 they moved to Cincinnati, then a small but flourishing town on the Ohio River. The trip from New York was made by canal boat, stage coach, and riverboat.

The family had barely settled in Cincinnati when Mr. Blackwell died, leaving his wife and nine children in straitened circumstances. Henry, the oldest son, quickly found work at the Cincinnati courthouse, but his earnings were not sufficient to maintain the household. It was essential that the three oldest girls—Anna, Marian, and Elizabeth—do something. But what?

As John Blake of the National Library of Medicine has observed: "The only careers open to an educated woman were writing, for which few of either sex have adequate talent, and teaching. As school boards found out they could hire women for one-half or less of the pay demanded by men, it dawned on them that women were after all the natural teachers of the young. . . . Many leaders of the women's rights movement, many of the country's first women doctors, started out in a teaching career."[3]

The Blackwell girls opened a boarding school for young ladies. Elizabeth, aged seventeen and slightly over five feet in height, became the disciplinarian. Four years later the two oldest boys were sufficiently well established in business to take care of the family's needs, and the sisters closed the school.

By then Elizabeth was "one of the new generation of discontented women" and was intrigued by the problems of female education.[4] She took private pupils until 1844, when she received an offer to organize a girls' school at Henderson, Kentucky. She was quick to accept but remained at Henderson only for one term. Living in direct contact with slavery proved too much for Elizabeth the abolitionist.

"I dislike slavery more and more every day," she wrote on April 4, 1844. "I suppose I see it here in its mildest form . . . but to live in the midst of beings degraded to the utmost in body and mind, drudging on from earliest morning to late at night, cuffed about by everyone, scolded at all day long, blamed unjustly, and without spirit enough to reply, with no consideration in any way for their feelings, with no hope for the future, smelling horribly, and as ugly as Satan —to live in their midst, utterly unable to help them, is to me dreadful, and what I would not do long for any consideration."[5]

She resigned her post. Back in Cincinnati were the Beechers, the Stowes, and the Channings, who thought and felt as she did.

DECISION ON A CAREER

It was not long after her return to Cincinnati that a friend dying of cancer said to her: "You are fond of study, have health and leisure; why not study medicine? If I could have been treated by a lady doctor, my worst sufferings would have been spared me." Elizabeth repudiated the suggestion as an impossible one, saying that she "hated everything connected with the body, and could not bear the sight of a medical book."[6]

Elizabeth tried to put the suggestion out of her mind but it would not stay out. Not only was she an ardent advocate of women's rights but, in the year 1845, no woman had ever attended an American medical school. As she later wrote, "a force stronger than myself then and afterwards seemed to lead me on; a purpose was before me which I must inevitably seek to accomplish."[7]

Once she had made up her mind to break the tradition that excluded women from medicine the first step was to acquire money for her tuition. For two years she taught school, first in North Carolina and then in South Carolina. In Asheville the principal of the school, the Reverend John Dickson, formerly a doctor, lent her medical books. In Charleston, Dr. Samuel H. Dickson, a distinguished physician and a professor at the medical college, gave her free access to his extensive medical library, guiding her in a study of the basic medical sciences.

By the summer of 1847 Elizabeth was ready. Her first move was to Philadelphia, where she worked with Dr. Joseph Warrington in his office, attended his lectures, and studied anatomy at the private school of a Dr. Allan, also a Quaker. Entry into a medical college seemed impossible. Her only hope, some doctors suggested, was to disguise herself as a man and either enter a medical school in Philadelphia (where selected, trustworthy students would support her deception) or go to Paris to study. "Elizabeth, it is no use trying. Thee cannot gain admission to these schools," her Quaker adviser told her. "Thee must go to Paris and don masculine attire to gain the necessary knowledge."[8]

If Elizabeth had been ready to give serious thought to this suggestion, she would doubtless have been put off by the friend who described Paris as "a city of fearful immorality where every feeling will be outraged . . . where vice is the natural atmosphere."[9] But to Elizabeth Blackwell, fighting "a moral crusade, . . . a course of justice and common sense must be pursued in the light of day," both suggestions were totally unacceptable.[10]

Application went forth to every major medical school and every lesser school. Many did not even reply. The replies received were for the most part crisply negative. But on November 7, 1847, Elizabeth Blackwell's name was entered on the roll books of the medical department of Geneva University.

MEDICAL SCHOOL

At Geneva things turned out quite differently from what both students and faculty had expected. The faculty had feared that the students would hail Miss Blackwell's arrival as an excuse for more riotous behavior than was customary, and despite their "pledge . . . that no conduct of ours shall cause her regret," the students may well have had something in mind. But Elizabeth—diffident and retiring but firmly determined—quickly won their admiration and even their affection. One of her classmates, Dr. Stephen Smith, was to report years later: "For the first time a lecture was given without the slightest interruption, and every word could be heard as distinctly as it would if there had been but a single person in the room. The sudden transformation of this class from a band of lawless desperadoes to gentlemen, by the mere presence of a lady, proved to be permanent in its effect."[11]

Within a week or two of her arrival the professor of anatomy, Dr. James Webster, requested that she remain out of his class for a few days because he would be lecturing on the reproductive system. Elizabeth replied with a carefully worded letter. The study of anatomy was a serious one, she wrote. All branches of it reflected glory on the Creator. She could not therefore imagine that a dedicated man of science would be disturbed by the fact that Student No. 130 wore a bonnet. But if it would distract him less, she would be delighted to remove her conspicuous headgear and sit in the back row. The lectures on anatomy proceeded in regular order, and Dr. Webster became her staunch friend. In fact, when Dr. Lee recoiled from the idea of a woman practicing surgery, Dr. Webster firmly supported her right to do so.

If classmates and faculty accepted her presence without question, not so the good people of Geneva. They considered her either a disreputable woman or a lunatic. Elizabeth was too busy to pay attention to their attempts at ostracism, but in their attitude she recognized a foretaste of the prejudice she would later encounter.

In January 1849 Elizabeth Blackwell was to take her final examinations. If she passed them, she would be entitled to the degree of Doctor of Medicine. The university administration panicked. If it conferred a doctorate in medicine on a woman, the school would be made a laughingstock, it said. Dr. Webster thundered in Elizabeth's defense. She had paid her fees and completed all required courses. What more could be asked of her? The administration wavered. Finally, when examination results revealed that she had achieved the highest average in the class, it capitulated. On January 23, 1849, the degree of Doctor of Medicine was awarded her by Dr. Hale.

Elizabeth's attendance at and graduation from Geneva had come about through chance and did not establish a precedent. Only one other woman ever graduated from its medical school—Mary Rogers in 1865. Even Emily Blackwell (1826–1910), Elizabeth's sister, was refused admission.

STUDIES ABROAD

It did not take long for Dr. Elizabeth Blackwell to recognize that, while an M.D. degree from Geneva was all a man might need successfully to enter practice, it would not suffice for a woman. She decided to visit England and then undertake additional medical studies in France.

Her stay in London was something of a triumph. Her accomplishments had been well publicized, in and out of the profession. There was a round of parties. There were lectures to attend and hospitals to be visited.

Her arrival in Paris was a severe letdown. No one had heard of her. When the French doctors learned that Dr. Blackwell planned to study at the general hospitals in Paris they were categorically opposed to the idea. The only institution open to her was La Maternité, an obstetrical center at which girls from all parts of France were trained as midwives. Since Elizabeth's degree did not exist in the eyes of the authorities, her only way into the institution was that of any eighteen-year-old student midwife. This meant that she would be rigidly supervised, practically imprisoned, and required to perform menial tasks.

Elizabeth did not hesitate. What difference did status make when set against an opportunity to study obstetrics in a hospital where three thousand babies were born each year? She was befriended by the senior intern, Hippolyte Blot, who showed her his unusual cases, gave her special instruction, and introduced her to exciting discoveries being made by French scientists.

On November 4, 1849, an incident occurred that almost terminated her career at its outset. While she was treating a baby with acute inflammation of the eye, a drop of infected liquid splashed back into her own left eye. By evening her eye was swollen and shut. Since there was at that time no sure treatment for severe eye infection, it was questionable whether either eye could be saved. For three weeks Elizabeth lay in darkness, under the care of Dr. Blot. In time the right eye healed. Nothing could be done about the other, which had to be removed some years later to avoid further infection of the right eye.

Many months passed before she could even use her right eye for reading. By then she knew that she must abandon her hope of becoming a surgeon. Ironically the repentant French doctors now invited her to attend clinics and lectures at any hospital she might select. Instead, following a rest cure at Gräfenberg, Germany, she returned to London at the beginning of October 1850. Here she was "granted permission to study in any ward, and follow the visit of any physician or surgeon at St. Bartholomew's Hospital who was willing to extend . . . the facilities of his department."[12] The only department to which she was refused admission was that of female diseases. She attended lectures at the hospital, including those on pathological anatomy given by James Paget. Henry James Bigelow, the noted New England surgeon, considered the Paget lectures so important that he traveled weekly from Paris to London to hear them.

It was at this time that Elizabeth Blackwell met Florence Nightingale, younger daughter of a wealthy upper-class family. It seemed unlikely to Dr. Blackwell that Florence would ever break the shackles put on her by birth and social standing. Later, Dr. Blackwell acknowledged that to Florence Nightingale she chiefly "owed the awakening to the fact that sanitation is the supreme goal of medicine, its foundation and its crown."[13]

Dr. Blackwell seriously considered establishing herself in London but she "was extremely poor, with no capital to fall back on, and with a great horror of running into debt."[14] On July 27, 1851, she sailed for New York. Here her plan to establish herself in practice turned out to be more difficult than she had realized. The first problem was office space. There were plenty of "rooms for rent"; but when landladies learned the use to which the rooms were to be put were they were quick to shut doors in her face. She was forced to rent an entire floor in a boarding house—more than she needed or could afford—because, in the words of the landlady, "no one else could be asked to share a floor with a female doctor."[15]

Dr. Blackwell now had an office but no patients. Her discreet shingle brought only abusive letters, telling her she was not wanted in the neighborhood. Attempts to find a place on the staff of a hospital proved equally fruitless. Qualifications meant nothing. She was a woman.

Elizabeth, with many unfilled hours on her hands, set about writing a series of lectures on the physical education of girls. This subject had interested the Blackwell sisters as far back as their days in Bristol. When the series was ready, she rented a church basement and placed a modest advertisement in the *New York Times*. This step was a turning point in her professional life.

The attending audience was small, but it was an intelligent one that included an influential group of Quaker women. Not only were they struck by the enlightened ideas of this woman doctor, but they agreed with her common-sense views on clothing, nutrition, exercise, and education. As a result she soon had a small private practice of well-to-do patients. But she regarded this success as only a step toward her goals for which she had worked so hard. She had a driving mission—to treat the underprivileged, the women and children of the slums. The hospitals and dispensaries made some attempt to take care of them, but she did not think they were doing enough; besides, she was barred from working through them. With the financial aid of some friends, she opened a small office near Tompkins Square on the Lower East Side, one of the worst areas, where she was available three days a week (and nights as needed) to those the city did not reach. Out of this small beginning grew the New York Dispensary for Poor Women and Children, incorporated in 1854.

COLLEAGUES AND PROJECTS

Now that Elizabeth was well established she encouraged her sister Emily to go into medicine. Emily's path was no easier. She attended Rush Medical College in Chicago during 1852–53 but was barred from continuing by the Illinois State Medical Society. When at the opening of the 1853–54 session the faculty of the Cleveland Medical College gave the dean "discretion in admission of female students,"[16] Emily took immediate advantage of the loophole. She graduated in 1854, one of two women in the class, and then went on to Edinburgh to study obstetrics under Sir James Y. Simpson, obstetrician to Queen Victoria.

Shortly after her return to New York in 1856 (in time to help Elizabeth with her latest venture), Sir James wrote to Emily: "I have rarely met with a young physician who was better acquainted with ancient and modern languages, or more learned in the literature, science, and practical details of his profession. Permit me to add that in your relationship to patients and in your kindly care and treatment of them I have ever found you a most womanly woman."[17]

While Emily had been abroad, the woman who became a third member of the team arrived unannounced on Elizabeth's doorstep: Marie E. Zakrzewska (1829–1902), a twenty-six-year-old Polish woman, who had been chief midwife at the Charité in Berlin. Three generations of women in her family had been famous midwives. Marie, in America to study medicine, had faced the usual discouragements. Advised by German doctors to go into nursing, she became the more determined to stick to her plans. But soon her money ran out. Someone at the Home for the Friendless suggested she see Dr. Blackwell.

Impressed by Marie, Dr. Blackwell invited her to work at the dispensary. She coached her in English, which Marie spoke haltingly, and arranged for her to go to medical school. To Emily, on May 12, 1854, Elizabeth wrote: "There is true stuff in her, and I shall do my best to bring it out. She must obtain a medical degree."[18] In

1856 Marie received her M.D. degree from Cleveland Medical College, one of four women in the class.

On May 12, 1857, Dr. Blackwell realized one of her goals. After a whirlwind of fund raising led by Dr. Zak (as Marie Zakrzewska came to be known), the New York Infirmary for Women and Children opened in Greenwich Village. It was the first true "Woman's Hospital in the world," according to Marie.[19] Despite the fact that angry mobs stormed the building on two occasions when a patient lay dying inside, the Blackwell sisters and Dr. Zak treated over three thousand patients the first year. The idea of a hospital run entirely by women shocked a great many people, but Elizabeth had solid Quaker support.

The hospital fulfilled another of Dr. Elizabeth's goals. Though by 1857 it was somewhat less difficult for a woman to attain an M.D. degree, too many promising careers ended at graduation because no hospital in the country would accept women as interns and residents. The New York Infirmary offered women doctors an opportunity to gain practical experience. From 1868 to 1899 it ran its medical school for women as well.

RETURN TO ENGLAND

Since Dr. Blackwell's stay in England in 1850–51 she had dreamed of practicing in the land of her birth. While she worked in New York she kept in touch with British medical regulations and had advance notice of the Medical Act of 1858. Among other things, this legislation provided that physicians with foreign degrees might register without examination if they were in active practice in Great Britain prior to October 1858. She returned to England in August 1858 in time to establish herself in practice and take advantage of the act. She had "the satisfaction of being enrolled as a recognized physician of [her] native land in the Medical Register of January 1, 1859."[20] On March 2 she lectured at the Marylebone Institute on the medical education of women. She was the first woman doctor to be recognized in Britain.

Dr. Blackwell would happily have remained in England, but the infirmary called her back. She remained in New York until the medical school was launched and she was able to retire from active participation in the now flourishing projects she had sponsored.

Dr. Emily Blackwell carried on the work that had been started. She served as president of the medical board of the infirmary and as dean of the medical school from 1869 to 1899. According to the medical educator Frederick C. Waite: "Dr. Elizabeth Blackwell is more widely known because of priority in graduation, but the younger sister was better educated, did most of the administrative work in the New York institutions, and was the first woman physician to engage extensively in major surgery."[21]

In 1869 Elizabeth returned to her beloved England. There she wrote and lectured on social and moral aspects of medicine. She died at the age of eighty-nine, having devoted her life to "those moral ends for which [she] took up the study of medicine."[22]

7. Elizabeth Garrett Anderson

In the mid-1850s the outlook for an unmarried woman who did not happen to be independently wealthy was still a grim one. She could either suffer through life as an unwanted poor relation or she could attempt to work for a living. For genteel ladies of the upper and middle classes, however, the opportunity to work was limited. They could be paid companions, occupying a role in the household of the employer somewhere between an inferior family member and a superior servant, or they could be governesses.

One of the goals of the growing women's rights movement in England was to attain relief from this status. As early as 1792 Mary Wollstonecraft (1759–1797) had written *A Vindication of the Rights of Women*. "It is time," she said, "to strike a revolution in female manners: to restore their lost dignity and make them labour, and by reforming themselves reform the world. . . . Women might certainly study the art of healing and be physicians as well as nurses."[1] An England in which women were considered to have no rights was profoundly shocked at the idea, and for fifty years after Mary Wollstonecraft's death nothing happened. But in 1859 Madame Bodichon (1827–1891), born Barbara Leigh Smith, rented rooms in Langham Place, London, and opened the first employment agency to handle white-collar jobs for women. The agency attracted not only single "ladies" who needed work but also girls dissatisfied with a life of idleness in the familial home.

Among the latter was Elizabeth Garrett (1836–1917), second of ten children of Newson Garrett, a prosperous businessman of Aldeburgh, Suffolk, and the former Louisa Dunnell. Like Samuel Blackwell, Mr. Garrett believed his children should have a better-than-average education.

At twenty-three Elizabeth's life at home was an extremely pleasant one, but she felt that she should make use of her ability and education. She was encouraged by an old schoolfriend, Emily Davies (1830–1921), who had long believed that women must be given the opportunity to obtain a better education and that the professions, especially medicine, should be opened to them. Emily Davies did not feel that she herself was "suited to be a pioneer in medicine; for this part of her programme she needed a lieutenant."[2] Her personal objective was to achieve good girls' schools with qualified teachers and the admission of women to public examination and to the universities.

A DECISION IS MADE

In 1859 Elizabeth stopped over in London to see an older sister before going on to visit Emily at Gateshead, where her father was the rector. During her stay she met Elizabeth Blackwell, just enrolled on the Medical Register, at Madame Bodichon's, and then attended her series of three lectures on "Medicine as a Profession for Ladies."

At this time Elizabeth Garrett was in no sense committed to a career in medicine, but Dr. Blackwell jumped to the conclusion that she had already made up her mind, and the younger woman was too overwhelmed to set her straight. "I remember feeling very much confounded and as if I had been suddenly thrust into work that was too big for me," she wrote later; while Dr. Blackwell recalled Miss Garrett as a "bright intelligent young lady whose interest in the study of medicine was then aroused."[3]

When Elizabeth Garrett reached Gateshead she was still undecided. Emily Davies weighted the scales of decision. "Now that you mention it, Elizabeth, I believe you *are* the ideal person to introduce the women of England to the medical profession," she said.[4]

When Elizabeth informed her parents of her intentions, Mr. Garrett was surprised and puzzled. "He does not *like* it, I think," she wrote Emily Davies, "or at least he would prefer my settling down into a douce young lady with no awkward energies. . . ."[5]

Mr. Garrett was a fair man. He told his daughter that, while he did not approve of her plans and would not actively support them, he would not stand in her way. Then he relented to the extent of accompanying his daughter on a round of visits to prominent Harley Street consultants in search of advice. In 1860 it would have been shocking for her to have gone alone.

The reception they received was anything but warm. These leaders of the profession were quick to point out that the medical education of a woman would be a waste of time since the name of a woman would never be entered on the Medical Register. Without this endorsement Miss Garrett would never be able legally to practice medicine in England.

Their position challenged Mr. Garrett's belief in equal education for men and women. He was quick to protest—his daughter had told him that Elizabeth Blackwell's name had been entered in the Medical Register earlier in the year. His objections were met by the statement: "Foreign degrees are no longer accepted, as they were when that woman from America entered the Register. *And no British examining board will ever admit a woman to its examinations.*"[6] (License by an examining board was a prerequisite to enrollment on the Register.)

This reception was swinging Mr. Garrett from his neutral position. When one doctor asked Elizabeth why she did not become a nurse instead of a doctor and she snapped back, "Because I prefer to earn a thousand rather than twenty pounds a year!" he was completely won over.[7]

Emily Davies once more acted as a catalyst. Her friend Emilia Batten was married to Russell Gurney, the Recorder of London, and

the Gurneys were friends of Dr. Blackwell's. When the latter had
to return to America in 1859, they had promised to see any woman
who might present herself for medical training. A meeting between
them and Elizabeth Garrett was arranged by Emily Davies' brother
John Llewelyn, rector of Christ Church Marylebone.

This contact was a happy one. "Mr. and Mrs. Gurney were extremely kind and helpful this morning," Elizabeth wrote Emily on
July 4, 1860, "and we have found someone who can be relied upon
to give Father a strongly favourable opinion of the movement.
. . . Mr. Gurney spoke of William Hawes and I found that Mr.
Hawes is the same that my father knows very well. They did a great
deal of business together a few years ago and I am pretty sure that
his opinion will have weight. . . ."[8]

Mr. Hawes was a member of the board of directors of Middlesex
Hospital. He offered a practical suggestion. Before Miss Garrett
faced the rigors, prejudices, and even persecutions she would meet
in medical school, why not first make sure that a life in medicine was
really for her? He proposed that she work for six months as a nurse
in the surgical ward of the hospital. Mr. Hawes believed that the
sights, sounds, and smells of a surgical ward would offer a searching
test. Elizabeth jumped at the opportunity. Middlesex was one of
London's great teaching hospitals. She would enter as a nurse and
then do everything possible to turn herself into a medical student.

AT MIDDLESEX HOSPITAL

A high degree of intelligence was not common in the nurses of the
day. Mrs. Yarrow, the matron (or head nurse), was delighted with
this recruit who not only understood orders but unfailingly carried
them out. Her charm and tact quickly brought the good will of her
fellow nurses, who had expected her to ignore or look down on them.
Best of all was the impression she made on the medical staff of the
hospital, especially on the dean of the medical school, T. W. Nunn,
and senior resident physician Willis. To them she confided her objec-

tive in working at the hospital, and they did whatever they could to help her. They arranged for her to be present at surgical operations, to join the medical students on rounds, and to see a great variety of cases passing through the out-patient clinic. Elizabeth's decision to embark on a career in medicine had been largely directed at further-ing the cause of equal education for women. Now she came to love the work for its own sake.

Her next step was to offer to pay the fees charged medical stu-dents, arguing that she was actually spending more time as a medical student than as a nurse. She believed that if a student fee was accepted from her she must automatically be recognized as a full-fledged medical student. The hospital administration did not fall into the trap. Miss Garrett was informed that the hospital was delighted to have her learn all she could—but strictly as an amateur. Nonethe-less she was given "the temporary use of a very pleasant room" in which she could read and keep her things. She asked Mr. De Mor-gan, the hospital treasurer, whether she might not someday be ac-cepted as a student. He replied that this would never happen in England; certainly none of the London colleges would admit her. If she were intent on becoming a medical student she should go to America. "I shall make every effort, however, to get the education in England and in the regular way though I believe much may be done irregularly," Elizabeth concluded.[9]

While Elizabeth was learning a great deal through observation she was barred from lectures. Her father came to the rescue. He offered to foot the bill for as many tutors as might be willing to instruct her. She gave up all pretense at being a nurse. Her time at the hospital was devoted to clinical study under the direction of her tutors.

Slowly she gained admission to lectures. She accomplished this by approaching the professors one by one, asking them in a charming, self-effacing manner if they would object to her presence. Few did. Here was a modest, singleminded woman trying to get along. She certainly was not one of those militant feminists whose manner of dress itself was an offense to decency. Elizabeth Garrett reminded them of their daughters and sisters—as they conceived them to be. Only the professor of anatomy feared to subject a genteel young lady to the ribald behavior of his students in the dissection room. But by the end of her first year at Middlesex she had won him over too.

Elizabeth's unofficial status was ended on petition of the male students. The fact that she had received honor grades in every course she had taken was kept secret from them, but when, in a burst of overenthusiasm one day on rounds she correctly answered a question that had been muffed by the rest, resentment was aroused. It was one thing to tolerate an attractive woman playing doctor but quite another to be made fools of in front of a visiting physician. The top students rallied to her defense, but in June 1861 she was informed that the Medical Committee had decided that the school would suffer from the presence of women at lectures. However, the "lecturers regretted that this decision had been arrived at 'in the case of a young lady whose conduct had, during her entire stay at the hospital, been marked by a union of judgement and delicacy which had commanded their entire esteem.' "[10]

A ROUNDABOUT APPROACH

Backed by her father, Elizabeth now tried to get into one of the great universities. Oxford and Cambridge would not even discuss the matter. Prospects at the University of London looked faintly brighter. Its charter clearly stated that it existed to provide education for "all classes and denominations without distinction whatsoever."[11] Her application, based on this provision, was rejected on the grounds that women were neither a class nor a denomination. On May 8, 1862, she wrote Dr. Blackwell: "I do not imagine there is much chance of being able to do more at any other university in the United Kingdom so that I fear the possibility of ever obtaining an English degree as M.D. is a very remote one."[12]

Since she was determined on being a licensed practitioner and no road to an M.D. degree appeared to be open, she and her father sought and found another method of entry to the Medical Register. The Society of Apothecaries conferred the degree of Licentiate of the Society of Apothecaries—L.S.A. This did not carry the prestige of an M.D. degree, but its recipients were duly accredited physicians with their names entered in the Medical Register. "My notion now is to try to get into a school and obtain the Apothecaries' Hall license," Elizabeth wrote Dr. Blackwell. But she viewed the approach as a compromise. "My own feeling is in favour of having the M.D., though it should be a foreign one I believe it would command more respect than the licence from the Hall would alone."[13]

The charter of the Society of Apothecaries provided that all persons who had served a five-year apprenticeship under a qualified doctor and taken certain prescribed lecture courses were eligible to take the qualifying examination. It would be hard to deny that Miss Garrett was a person, and the Apothecaries did not attempt it. On August 17, 1861, they told Miss Garrett to come back when she had fulfilled the requirements. They were satisfied that she would not return; so attractive a young lady would be married and raising a family before five years had passed. They reckoned without Elizabeth Garrett's perseverance.

The apprenticeship was easy. Joshua Plaskitt, one of her special tutors while at Middlesex, was now in private practice. He was happy to sponsor her. The lectures were something else. She was able to obtain certificates for the lectures she had attended at Middlesex, but for the rest she again had to gain admission to some university. Having exhausted English possibilities, she turned to Scotland.

She almost was enrolled at St. Andrews University. An aging clerk, a Mr. MacBean, accepted a matriculation fee of one pound and had her write her name in the university ledger. This act made Elizabeth Garrett a member of the university. Surely she could not now be refused admission to medical lectures. But the Senate of the university ordered Mr. MacBean to return the fee. Elizabeth accepted it from him and promptly mailed it back to the Senate, "adding a letter to say that till the question was decided legally against my being allowed to retain the matriculation ticket, I could not consent to have the fee paid for same returned to me."[14] Mr. Garrett threatened suit. Official opinion was divided. The Solicitor-General and Attorney-General, Sir Fitzroy Kelly, declared that the Senate could not admit a woman even if it wished to do so. On the other hand, James Moncrieff, Lord Advocate for Scotland, held that the charter did not make it impossible for a woman to attend college classes. However, he conceded, the Senate had considerable discretionary power and might refuse anyone it chose, male or female. The Senate stood its ground. Mr. Garrett and Elizabeth decided that the publicity of a lawsuit might do their cause more harm than good. Elizabeth remained at St. Andrews for a semester, working privately with Professor Day, Regius Professor of Medicine, who had encouraged her attempt to matriculate. She acquired one more precious certificate.

Her next assault, on the University of Edinburgh, also failed, but she spent the summer of 1863 in Edinburgh, working under Sir James Simpson, with whom Emily Blackwell had studied after her graduation from medical school in 1854. Sir James, a great admirer of Dr. Emily Blackwell, was exceptional in his faith in women doctors.

Elizabeth's attempt to find a lecturer of an acknowledged school of medicine who would train her in dissection and surgical anatomy involved letters to doctors as far as Aberdeen in the Scottish Highlands. At last, in February 1864, she was given permission to visit the wards of London Hospital, under the pretext of being a nurse in the obstetrical department. Here she was also able to study under the professor of anatomy in the medical school. Resentment of her presence apparently developed soon after her appearance at the hospital and drove her out in October. "They seem to have dwelt particularly on the shabbiness of my pretending to be a nurse," she wrote Emily Davies, "but I said it was not my fault, I had given them two chances of having me as a regular student."[15]

She returned to Middlesex Hospital, where she was given no

general permission to visit wards, but "each physician and surgeon had power to grant permission at his discretion for his own wards or ward."[16] This unsatisfactory arrangement continued until March 1865.

"ELIZABETH GARRETT—L.S.A."

Piece by piece Elizabeth had put together the required education. In the fall of 1865 she presented to a shocked Society of Apothecaries proof that she had met all requirements. The examining body of the society balked. Naturally they hadn't meant what they had said. They couldn't possibly admit Miss Garrett to their examination.

This was the final straw for Newson Garrett. He threatened to sue if it took every penny he possessed. On the advice of their lawyers the Apothecaries backed down. In September, Elizabeth took the examination, which turned out to be ridiculously easy. In 1866 the name of Elizabeth Garrett, L.S.A. was officially entered in the Medical Register.

First Elizabeth Blackwell, English-born but American bred, had found her way in through her foreign degree. That loophole had been closed immediately. Now Elizabeth Garrett—English throughout—had sneaked in on the technicality that women were persons. It would not happen again. The Apothecaries voted themselves a new charter that required graduation from an accredited medical school as a prerequisite for the L.S.A. degree. Since women were excluded from such schools, the Medical Register of England was doubly closed to them.

In 1865 Mr. Garrett leased and furnished for Elizabeth a house at No. 20 Upper Berkeley Street. Her shingle read: ELIZABETH GARRETT, L.S.A. "I don't like 'Miss Garrett' on the door," she wrote. "It is only like a dressmaker."[17]

Her private practice was successful from the start. In addition she established a small clinic, St. Mary's Dispensary for Women. Here she saw sixty to ninety women from the surrounding slum area three afternoons a week. The clinic was to grow into the New Hospital for Women, which was renamed the Elizabeth Garrett Anderson Hospital in 1917.

She still needed a staff position at a regular hospital. An opportunity appeared in 1869 when a vacancy occurred at the Shadwell Hospital for Children (subsequently the Princess Elizabeth of York Hospital for Children). One member of the hospital board of directors, and a generous contributor to its activities, was a handsome Scottish bachelor, head of a large shipping firm—James George Skelton Anderson. He came to the meeting with his mind already made up. He would listen politely to the recital of the qualifications of Miss Garrett, L.S.A., and then exercise his right of veto. He reversed himself after watching her and listening to her replies. She received her hospital appointment and within two years was married to Mr. Anderson.

ELIZABETH GARRETT, M.D.

Elizabeth was sensitive about being merely Miss Garrett, L.S.A. She informed one writer who had incorrectly addressed her, "I have no claim to the title of *Dr.* Elizabeth, and I do not like to have that which does not of right belong to me."[18]

A year earlier, in 1868, the University of Paris had made its medical degrees available to women. Miss Garrett decided to sit for the examination for a Paris degree, provided she was given permission to do so without first living in Paris as a student.

Through the British Ambassador in Paris, Lord Lyons, she gained the necessary permission. By June 1870 she was legally entitled to write M.D. after her name. While she continued to practice in London as an L.S.A., her diploma from the University of Paris unquestionably raised her professional standing.

Without neglecting her duties as a devoted wife and the mother of two children, she continued to pioneer in medicine and education.

In 1878 she performed what was believed to be the first surgical removal of an ovary successfully undertaken by a woman. She served from 1883 to 1903 as dean of the London School of Medicine for Women, which had been established in 1874. She was also active in the British Medical Association.

MEMBER OF THE BRITISH MEDICAL ASSOCIATION

The records of the British Medical Association note that Dr. Elizabeth Garrett was "inadvertently"[19] admitted to membership by the Paddington (London) branch in 1873, a fact that did not become generally known until 1875, when she was scheduled to read a paper at the annual meeting in Edinburgh. Sir Robert Christison, then president of the association, was rabid in his objection to medical women. He could do nothing about Dr. Garrett, since her membership was legal and could not be annulled. Proper procedural steps were then taken to exclude any further women applicants. A plebiscite covering 6230 members brought 4161 replies, of which 3072 favored exclusion.

At the 1878 meeting a clause was added to the articles of the association stating: "No female shall be eligible for election as a member of the Association."[20] This clause was not repealed until 1892, when three or four members only voted for its continuance.[21]

For nineteen years Dr. Garrett was the only woman member. She regularly attended meetings, usually spoke at them, and held a number of offices.

RETIREMENT

In 1902 the Andersons retired to the Garrett family home in Aldeburgh. After her husband's death in 1907 she was elected mayor —certainly an unusual accomplishment at that time.

As Dr. Brunton has said: "There is no question that she did more for the cause of women in medicine in England than any other person." Others were "of a more fiery nature and frequently got . . . into hot water. . . . The more balanced outlook and quieter perseverance of Elizabeth Garrett went very much further in advancing the cause of women."[22]

8. The Battle
for Recognition at Home

In the period from the 1850s to the early 1900s women made slow but steady progress toward their goal of a medical education and a place in the medical profession. Until the university medical schools were opened to women on an equal footing, another solution had to be found.

THE WOMEN'S MEDICAL COLLEGES

As early as 1842 a group of Philadelphia physicians, including several Quakers, talked of establishing a medical school for women. The project remained little more than a dream until 1848, when plans began to take shape under the urging of Dr. Joseph S. Longshore. Such a school was of particular interest to the Longshore family, for Dr. Longshore's sister, Anna Mary Longshore, and his sister-in-law, Hannah Myers Longshore, were serving apprenticeships at his clinic; lacking diplomas, they foresaw little or no opportunity to practice medicine, especially in Philadelphia.

The Female Medical College of Pennsylvania, incorporated in 1850, was the world's first chartered medical school for women. The original faculty consisted of six medical men—among them Dr. Longshore and Dr. Bartholomew Fussell, a Quaker physician. All of them showed considerable moral courage since they were faced by prejudice and professional hostility.

It would have been appropriate for a woman to have been included on the faculty, but in 1850 there were only two women with medical degrees, Elizabeth Blackwell and Lydia Folger Fowler. Dr. Blackwell does not appear to have been aware of the plans for the college. This is somewhat surprising in view of her having studied in Philadelphia in 1847 and worked there at the Blockley almshouse in the summer of 1848. In any event she was in Europe when the Philadelphia school opened. Dr. Fowler was committed to teach at Rochester.

The 1850 enrollment of forty women included eight who intended to work for an M.D. degree. Hannah Myers Longshore, who graduated in December 1851, entered private practice in Philadelphia and also taught at the college.

The state and local medical societies did their utmost to crush the upstart institution. Resolutions were passed against the professors on the grounds that some of them were irregular practitioners, and against women in general as being "unfit for medicine."[1] Ann Preston, one of the school's early graduates, a mild-mannered Quaker, led the fight against the societies. When, after a brief period of inactivity due to the Civil War, the school reopened as the Women's Medical College of Pennsylvania, she became the dean.

This change of name reflected no departure from its original purposes. "The college kept pace with advancing science. . . . Like most medical schools of this period, [it] had practically no endowment and no aid from the state, medical science not yet having proved so useful as to elicit from a practical-minded society either private or public support. Since all professors were engaged in private practice, however, the college did not have to worry about salaries; the laboratory facilities were as yet relatively inexpensive."[2] By the early 1890s the faculty numbered sixty-six, about half of whom were women.

The college functioned for a hundred and twenty years as a medical school for women. Among its graduates were a number of women who broke ground for others: Clara Swain, class of 1869, was the first medical missionary, serving in India; Anandibai Joshee, 1866, from India; Constance Stone, 1887, from Australia; and Susan LaFlesche Picotte, daughter of a chief of the Omaha tribe, 1889.

Nineteen medical schools for women were established between 1850 and 1895 in Boston, New York, Baltimore, and other cities. The New England Female Medical College, successor to the Boston Female Medical College (it had been little more than a school for midwives despite its name), was chartered in 1856 and entitled to confer medical degrees. The school was the first to grant a medical degree to a black woman, Rebecca Lee, in 1864. In 1874 it merged with the then homeopathic medical department of Boston University to form a coeducational department.

The New York Medical College and Hospital for Women was opened by Dr. Clemence S. Lozier in 1863. Among its graduates were Emily Jennings Stone, class of 1867, from Canada, and Marie Augusta Generoso Estrela of Brazil, 1881.

As Dr. Shryock writes, "By 1870 it was clear that women in medicine had come to stay, but there remained much uncertainty as to their status. The next twenty years were ones of slow but continuous growth in the resources of the women's schools and in the number of their graduates. Teaching was improved by expanding the small faculties, by securing access to general clinics, and by enlarging the women's hospitals."[3]

THE UNIVERSITIES OPEN THEIR DOORS

In 1873, when Lucy Wanzer applied for admission to Tolland Hall Medical School in San Francisco, she received the time-worn answer—medical school was no proper place for a woman—and she was advised to go to some eastern women's college. She persisted, and her case came before the board of regents. On the advice of their attorneys they ruled that "it is an organic law of the state that the male and female shall have equal choice in the University in all its departments."[4] In spite of the dean's suggestion to her fellow students that they "make it so uncomfortable for her that she cannot stay," she soon became well liked and went on to graduate.[5]

In 1879 the University of Michigan opened the doors of its medical school to women, followed by the universities of Iowa, Minnesota, Colorado, California, Oregon, Buffalo, Syracuse, Boston, the District of Columbia, and Johns Hopkins in Baltimore. The Cleveland Medical College, which, after having conferred degrees on Emily Blackwell, Marie Zakrzewska, and a few other women, had adopted a report by the American Medical Association against coeducation, adhered to its 1851 resolution against the admission of women until 1879. In 1881 the college merged with the University of Wooster (Ohio) to become the Medical Department of Western Reserve University.

COEDUCATION

In the early days of coeducation at Johns Hopkins, writes Dr. Shryock, "women students were allowed to examine men only above the neck—here male modesty entered the picture—with resulting embarrassment when women were later assigned to men's wards."[6] In 1893 Elizabeth Garrett Anderson endowed the school with close to half-a-million dollars on condition that it waive any restrictions on sex, making it, according to the noted educator Abraham Flexner, the first American medical school "of a genuine university type."[7]

By 1900 thirty-five to forty regular medical schools were admitting students of both sexes. The women's medical schools, having fulfilled their purpose, were either disbanded or merged with regular medical schools when admissions policies were no longer so restrictive. The Women's Medical College of the New York Infirmary for Women and Children closed in 1898 after twenty years' activity and its students were transferred to the newly opened Cornell Medical School.

There is some question as to whether eight or four women's

medical schools were still in operation in 1900—a difference of opinion as to just what constituted a women's medical college may account for the discrepancy.[8] By 1910, according to one source, only two remained, the Women's Medical College of Pennsylvania and a New York homeopathic institution; another source says that three schools existed in each of the years 1904 through 1909 and that the Women's Medical College of Baltimore, founded in 1882, was active through 1910.[9]

Coeducation was not only acceptable by now but preferable. In 1910 Dr. Flexner came out against separate medical schools, saying that "Large sums, as far as specially available for the medical education of women, would accomplish most if used to develop coeducational institutions, in which their benefits would be shared by men without loss to women students; but . . . if separate medical schools and hospitals are not to be developed for women, interne privileges must be granted to women on the same terms as to men."[10]

This last had long been a sore point with women graduates. Internships, residencies, and faculty appointments remained difficult to obtain, and the established ratio of women to men in coeducational classes was insufficient to take care of all qualified women applicants. Dr. Shryock, in speaking of "multiple lines of conservative defense" that precluded "the full admission of women into medicine" points out that if "one were scaled, the opposition reformed in the rear. If women could get into schools, the hospitals were still closed; and if the latter were finally opened, internships and residencies were still denied them. When 'doctoring ladies' appeared, physicians refused to consult with them and prevented their entrance into medical societies."[11]

THE MEDICAL SOCIETIES

Dr. Nancy Talbot Clarke's unsuccessful attempt to become a member of the Massachusetts Medical Society was made in 1853. The society continued to exclude women until 1884, when Dr.

Emma Louise Call of Boston, with a medical degree from the University of Michigan, was admitted.

Women doctors began knocking at the door of the Philadelphia County Medical Society in 1853. Most of the society's membership remained so opposed to women physicians that in 1868 the society decreed that its members should not consult with females and that, if any member accepted a chair on the faculty of the Woman's Medical College, he would forfeit his membership. It was not until thirteen years later, in 1881, that the society passed this resolution: *"Resolved* that female medical practitioners in good standing in the profession are eligible to membership in this society under the same laws and regulations now governing the admission of men."[12] However, no woman was actually admitted until seven years later. She was Dr. Mary Willets, a graduate of the Woman's Medical College of Pennsylvania. It is interesting to note that the first black doctor was also admitted in 1888.

The question of admitting women doctors to the then twenty-two-year-old American Medical Association first arose at a Washington meeting in 1868, but consideration of a resolution specifically endorsing women for membership was postponed indefinitely. Some members were rabid in their hostility. The 1871 *Transactions of the American Medical Association* recorded a statement by Alfred Stillé, a prominent teacher of pathology:

> Another disease has become epidemic. "The woman question" in relation to medicine is only one of the forms in which the *pestis muliebris* vexes the world. In other shapes it attacks the bar, wriggles into the jury box, and clearly means to mount upon the bench; it strives, thus far in vain, to serve at the altar and thunder from the pulpit; it raves at political meetings, harangues in the lecture-room, infects the masses with its poison, and even pierces the triple brass that surrounds the politician's heart.

> To the vulgar apprehension, nothing seems more natural

than that women should be physicians, for is not nursing the chief agent in the cure of disease, and who so fit a nurse as woman! The logic is worthy of its subject, and is of the sort in which Eve's daughters excel.[13]

A year later at Philadelphia the new president of the American Medical Association, Dr. David W. Yandell, mildly defended the rights of women to practice medicine if the public so wished, but he hoped that "they will never embarrass us by a personal application for seats in the Association.[14]

In 1876 Sarah Hackett Stevenson, a graduate of the Woman's Medical College of Chicago, gained admission to the association's meeting as a delegate from Illinois by signing the roll call "S. Stevenson." When her sex became apparent, it was moved that the names of female delegates be referred to the Judicial Council. The motion was laid on the table and remained there for almost forty years. Not until 1915 were women admitted to membership. The same year saw the formation of the Medical Women's National Association, later the American Medical Women's Association.

Actually the first society to admit women was that of Montgomery County (Pennsylvania). Its 1870 transactions state: "Norristown, May 1870. Doctress Anna Lukens was elected a member. This is the first female physician ever elected in a county society in Pennsylvania, or perhaps in the United States—perhaps the world. She was a pupil of Dr. Hiram Corson and is a graduate of the Woman's Medical College, Philadelphia."[15]

It would seem that women doctors should have an indisputable right to membership in an obstetrical society. After all, modern obstetrics was an outgrowth of midwifery, the province of women long before the advent of the man midwife. But even here they were at first excluded.

The founding of the Obstetrical Society of Philadelphia in 1868 was largely the work of Dr. Albert H. Smith, a Quaker and a strong supporter of the Woman's Medical College. It was clearly his intention to qualify women for membership in the society, but he recognized the need for moving slowly. Periodically at meetings of the society he read papers prepared by women physicians. At last, at a meeting on October 2, 1879, he presented this resolution: *"Moved* that when any physician in regular standing shall announce for presentation to a meeting of the Society through a member, a specimen for exhibition or paper to be read connected with the object of the Society, said Physician shall be considered a guest of the Society at such meeting and may be invited by the President to enter into discussion to which such presentation may give rise."[16]

The resolution was offered at the November meeting and seconded. In the discussion that followed, a member stated: "There being nothing to prevent the presence of women as visitors and only the impossibility of obtaining the necessary four-fifths votes prevents them from being members, as an expression of opinion I would take pleasure in voting for it. Women [have] already obtained admission to a number of medical societies and were valued members. Science should take no recognition of sex or color." Dr. William Goodell, a former president of the society, was opposed: "My education, my associations and feeling make it painful to me to meet women in this Society." Nine members voted in favor of Dr. Smith's resolution, eighteen against.[17]

For thirteen years the minutes of the society make no mention of women as guests or members. Then, on April 7, 1892, without preliminary fanfare, seven out of thirteen physicians admitted to membership were women. Their champion, Dr. Smith, had died in 1885. His dream had taken roughly a quarter of a century to become reality.

But what is a quarter of a century? The College of Physicians of Philadelphia, founded in 1787, survived a hundred and forty-five years as an exclusively male organization. When a move to admit women was initiated in 1929, the membership referred the matter to a lawyer, who took a full year to decide that the constitution of the college would permit such an admission. This being settled, the membership took another year deciding whether or not they wished to admit women. Then, since the constitution permitted it and the members now wished it, the question was who should the woman be. Dr. Martha Tracy, dean of the Woman's Medical College, was consulted. She proposed Dr. Catharine Macfarlane (1898–1969), research professor of gynecology, Women's Medical College of Pennsylvania.

"On the evening of January 11, 1932," Dr. Macfarlane wrote, ". . . I was admitted to membership. The President of the College, Dr. Francis R. Packard, the eminent otolaryngologist and medical historian, reached over to shake my hand and greeted me with the words 'You are making history tonight, Dr. Macfarlane.' "[18] In fact, Dr. Macfarlane had merely joined the ranks of the medical women, from Nancy Talbot Clarke on, who had made history by fighting for the acceptance of women as equal members of the medical community.

9. Progress
toward Equality Abroad

The advance started more slowly in England. There women who would be doctors were faced by opposing forces that seemingly could not be reconciled. They were excluded from the lecture room because they could not be examined; they could not be examined, the licensing bodies said, because they had not attended the prescribed lectures. As far as the practical aspects of medical training were concerned, Queen Victoria herself set the tone: she was horrified at the "awful idea" of young girls and men mingling in the dissecting room.

Sophia Jex-Blake (1840–1912), a fiery advocate of women's rights, particularly in the field of medicine, has been described by Dr. Brunton as "the type of person of whom it has been said, 'They are capable of first heating the water and then getting into it.' "[1] In the 1860s, under her leadership, "a handful of heroines made a gallant attempt to storm the University of Edinburgh. The siege lasted longer than that of Troy, the citadel being most obstinately defended by the garrison."[2] The opposition was led by the powerful and influential Sir Robert Christison, the British authority on toxicology, who was to be president of the British Medical Association when the awful fact of Elizabeth Garrett's membership was revealed in 1875.

In 1869 the Faculty of Medicine finally matriculated Sophia Jex-Blake and six other women; then, in 1871, refused to teach them and incited male students to take physical action against them. The students were said to have been led by Professor Christison's assistant. Miss Jex-Blake stated this in public, and Sir Robert sued her for libel. He was awarded one farthing—a quarter of a penny. In 1873 she brought suit against the ruling body of the university, asking for a declaration that the university must enable her and her fellow women students to complete their education and be examined for their degree in medicine. She won her case. On appeal, the verdict was reversed by a majority of one, and the women were forced to withdraw.

The way out of the dilemma seemed to lie in the establishment of an institution offering complete medical education to women. In 1874, under the patronage and guidance of Dr. Francis Austie and other liberal-minded and influential members of the profession, Sophia Jex-Blake founded the London School of Medicine for Women. It opened on October 12 with fourteen students.

No hospital was willing to serve as a teaching hospital for the students and there was no examining board to examine them. By February 1876 these deficiencies had led to the loss of several students, and it became clear that the school must close by the end of the year unless qualifying hospital practice could be arranged for.

Russell Gurney, who had helped Elizabeth Garrett get started on her medical education and who had since then become a member of Parliament, was active on behalf of women's rights. He had sponsored the Married Women's Property Act, designed to relieve wives of the almost literal bonds of matrimony; he was a prime mover in the establishment of the New Hospital for Women and the London School of Medicine for Women; and he introduced into Parliament a bill giving all medical examining boards the right to admit women to their examinations. This bill became law on August 12, 1876, as the Medical Act of 1876. While there continued to be some opposition from the universities, this was the turning point. The following year the Royal Free Hospital opened its wards to the students of the London School of Medicine for Women. The school maintained its independent status until 1901, when it became one of the colleges of the University of London.

One of its distinguished graduates was Christine Murrell (1874–1933), born the year the school was opened. Of her role Dr. Brunton has written: "The task of her forerunners was to establish the right of women to enter the profession. There remained the harder task of proving that they could be of value to it. It was this task that Christine Murrell accomplished with paramount success."[3] Her greatest contribution was in the field of public service. In those days it was laid down by men (and accepted by women) that the "weaker sex" was less healthy than the male. By teaching women about themselves, Dr. Murrell went a long way toward exploding this sophistry. She lectured to working girls and mothers on such topics as first aid, home nursing, and the care of infants. Above all, she was an advocate of public health through preventive medicine. She started a number of well-baby clinics that were operated essentially along the same lines as such clinics are run today.

As the century drew to a close it was hardly more difficult for a woman to get a complete medical education than it was for a man. Women could obtain degrees after examination in the ordinary way at the universities of London, Durham, Edinburgh, Glasgow, St. Andrews, and Ireland.

In Italy

Italy never had a law either enabling or forbidding women to enter its universities. Consequently it was more than a century ahead of the rest of the world in producing medical women of distinction.

Laura Maria Caterina Bassi (1711–1778) earned the degree of doctor of philosophy at Bologna in 1731 or 1732, became an authority on mechanics, hydraulics, natural history, and anatomy, and occupied the chair of anatomy until her marriage. Thereafter she devoted herself to family life, raising and educating twelve children.

Anna Morandi (1716–1774), born in Bologna, married the professor of anatomy at the university, Giovanni Mahzolini. She herself studied anatomy and produced wax models of dissected specimens colored to simulate the original. These teaching aids were an improvement over those developed four centuries earlier by Allessandra Giliani. Emperor Joseph II of Germany bought several of her models. During her husband's terminal illness, she lectured in his place and in 1760 succeeded him as professor of anatomy. Catherine II of Russia invited her to lecture in Moscow and made her a member of the Russian Royal Scientific Association. The British Royal Society also elected her a member.

At the University of Padua, Angiolina of Padua held the chair of obstetrics. Maria Petraccini, who is said to have obtained her degree in Florence, in 1780, and her daughter, Zaffira Ferreti (Bologna, 1800) both taught anatomy at Ferrara.

Maria delle Donne (1776–1842) received an M.D. degree from Bologna, where she "was unanimously invested with every honor the faculty had to distribute." Her ability was recognized by Napoleon. His attempt in 1802 to have her elected to the chair of physics failed, but he had her made professor of obstetrics. In 1807 he elevated her to the French Academy of Sciences. Meanwhile in 1804 she had become the director of the Bologna school of midwives. Of all the women medical teachers who "adorned that ancient seat of learning," Bologna, the most famous was Giuseppina Cattani, who was associated with Guido Tizzoni in his work on cholera in 1886.[4]

ELSEWHERE AROUND THE WORLD

Zurich, Switzerland, entered the first woman student on the register of its university medical faculty in 1864. The registrant was a Russian, who does not appear to have completed her studies, but she was quickly followed by another Russian, Nadeya Suslowa of St. Petersburg, who was granted her degree on December 14, 1867. Two Swiss women graduates, Marie Heim-Vögtlin (1845–1916) and Anna Heer (1862–1918) opened a training school for nurses in 1901 that would become famous for its high standards.

Paris did not open its doors to women until 1868. Madeleine Brès, in 1867, applied to the dean of the Faculty of Medicine for permission to enter. She was told that she must first produce the usual certifications of bachelor degrees in arts and sciences. These she submitted a year later. Her application was returned with a favorable answer. But there is no further word of Mlle. Brès, and it is not known if she was graduated.

German universities were the slowest in Europe to accept women as candidates for doctorates in medicine. Prussia was the last state to capitulate, in 1908.

Holland, like Italy, never had laws excluding women from its universities, but there was no rush to take advantage of this opportunity. Aletta Jacobs was apparently the first woman to study medicine formally, passing her state examinations in 1878. Catherine van Tussenbroek received a medical degree the same year.

Belgian medical schools were opened to women in 1883.

In the Scandinavian countries, Sweden opened its universities to women in 1873, Denmark in 1875, and Norway in 1882. In Finland, a woman was appointed municipal doctor at Helsingfors in 1882, and nine years later there were four women students of medicine at the University of Helsingfors.

In 1868, the Scientific Society of Russia petitioned the czar to allow women to study medicine. Four years later the petition was answered with the establishment at St. Petersburg of a Medical Faculty for Women. In the next ten years almost a thousand students were admitted to the school. Six hundred completed their studies and found employment in public sanitary and poor-law services, hospitals, asylums, schools, factories, and in private practice. In the Russo-Turkish War of 1877 advanced students of the school performed yeoman service and were commended by the Minister of War. For some reason the school was totally suppressed in August 1882. However, it was reopened in 1897.

The year 1887 seems to have been a year of breakthroughs. The University of Melbourne and the University of Sydney in Australia opened their doors to women medical students; and in Latin America, the University of Chile, the Faculty of Medicine of Bahía, Brazil, and the University of Mexico conferred their first medical degrees on women. Co-education in medicine was on the march, outside as well as inside the United States. By 1896 it was possible for a current periodical to say: "The walls of the medical Jericho are everywhere falling at the sound of the trumpet of the female Joshuas. The recent vote at the College of Physicians was a moral victory for them; the Council and the Fellows of the College of Surgeons are willing to admit them to the privilege of membership; all the other corporations give them their diplomas on the same terms as these are granted to men. . . . The portals of the profession stand open to them in all civilized countries except Germany and Austria."[5]

10. Mary Putnam Jacobi

The career of Mary Putnam Jacobi (1842–1906) bridges the traditional difficulties and the modern attitudes evolving in the last half of the nineteenth century.

Her decision to become a doctor came as a distasteful shock to all the Putnams except her immediate family. It had been taken for granted that she would be a writer. (Her father, George Palmer Putnam, was the publisher of such American immortals as Washington Irving, James Fenimore Cooper, Nathaniel Hawthorne, and Edgar Allan Poe.) Minnie, as she was called, began writing remarkably precocious letters and compositions when she was six years old. At seventeen she sold "Lost and Found," a story about the discovery of the source of the Nile, to the *Atlantic Monthly* for eighty dollars. In 1859 eighty dollars was a considerable sum of money. Dr. Victor Robinson, Ukranian-born American medical historian, wrote in 1928 that when he "read this tale years ago . . . [he] did not think it worth the price." He described a further contribution to the same magazine, "Hair-Chains," as "full of bathos rather than pathos," but he conceded that if she "had cultivated literature in her maturity, she would be known today as the forerunner of Edith Wharton, Willa Cather and Edna Ferber."[1] But this was not to be. Minnie had an inquisitive mind and had long been fascinated by anything to do with science. She announced her plans when she graduated from Miss Lydia Wadleigh's school for girls in New York. Medical schools in the city were not open to women, and, broadminded as he was, Mr. Putnam could not accept the thought of a young daughter living away from home. By way of compromise it was agreed that Minnie should take a one-and-a-half year course at the New York College of Pharmacy. She graduated in 1863, the first woman to graduate from the college and, as it turned out, the only woman to graduate until 1886.

Now that Minnie was twenty-one her father agreed to let her attend the Female Medical College of Pennsylvania. His parting request was that she not let herself be "absorbed and gobbled up in that branch of the animal kingdom ordinarily called strong-minded women!"[2] Life in Philadelphia was far from comfortable. Urged on by "organized medicine," male students of the local medical schools made life miserable for the girls of the Female Medical College.

As was customary among medical schools throughout the country, the college offered a two-year course. The same set of lectures was given in each of the two years, the theory apparently being that what was missed in the first year would be picked up in the second. Dr. Ann Preston, the dean, evidently impressed by Mary Putnam's prior education, allowed her to take her examinations at the end of one year. She received her degree in March of 1864.

The next move was to the New England Hospital for Women and Children. This internship was followed by graduate work in chemistry. Still, she felt that her education did not put her on a footing with graduates of the leading schools from which she and other women were barred. What she needed was a diploma from "the greatest university in the world." In September 1866 she sailed for Europe, determined to breach the reputedly impenetrable University of Paris. Elizabeth Blackwell, who was wintering in Paris, cautioned her to move carefully. The great Ecole de Médicine was not yet to be thought of.

Dr. Putnam rejected a suggestion (similar to that made earlier to Elizabeth Blackwell) "that she wear male attire, like the Grecian Agnodice," pleading "that trousers would only accentuate her littleness."[3] For the time being she satisfied herself with the permission of two doctors to join the students who followed them on their hospital rounds. She moved slowly toward her goal. Before the year was over she was allowed to attend an important clinic in surgery and the library of the School of Medicine was opened to her. She also gained admission to some lectures at the Ecole Pratique, only one step removed from the Ecole de Médicine itself.

Mary had been in Paris for a year and a half when she learned that the Minister of Public Instruction was anxious to see a woman enrolled at the School of Medicine. His was a lone voice. Her formal application for admission was turned down. There was, in fact, only one vote in her favor. There was nothing to do but wait until the next term and apply again.

Meanwhile, though the front door was barred, there was a back entrance. Mary obtained permission to take just one course, without credit. On January 25, 1868, she wrote her mother: "Day before yesterday, for the first time since its foundation several centuries ago a petticoat might be seen in the august amphitheatre of the Ecole de Médicine. That petticoat enrobed the form of your most obedient servant and dutiful daughter!"[4] By the time the next entrance examinations rolled around the petticoat had become an accustomed sight in the amphitheater. Her application to take the examinations, supported by the dean and four professors, was accepted. She passed with high honors.

For her thesis, she chose a biochemical theme, *De la graisse neutre et des acides gras* ("On Neutral Fats and Acids"). Her judges, though not qualified to discuss the subject, pronounced the thesis *extrèmement satisfait* and awarded her a Paris Faculty medal. She had dedicated her dissertation to "the professor, whose name I do not know, who was the only one to vote for my admission to the school, thus protesting against the prejudice which would exclude women from advanced studies." Relenting in face of the honor done her, she now inscribed several copies "To the Faculty of Paris, which in according the honor of a degree to women, has risen to the height of French liberality."[5]

On July 29, 1871, she wrote to her mother: "I have passed my last examination—oh, I told you. I have passed my thesis, and am now docteur en médicine de la Faculté de Paris."[6]

Dr. Putnam, now twenty-nine, returned home toward the end of 1871. After spending six years in Paris, this descendant of seven ancestors who fought at Bunker Hill had become so French that she could not talk English without interjecting French phrases.

In Paris she had promised Elizabeth Blackwell that, on her return to New York, she would teach at the Woman's Medical College of the New York Infirmary, which was being run by Dr. Emily Blackwell. The students resented the French style of teaching and complained that it made unreasonable demands on them. Dr. Emily, to whom they carried their objections, lacked her sister's affability and open-heartedness. She sided with the students. Dr. Putnam was informed that the school's standards were already higher than those of most medical schools and no French innovations were needed.

Dr. Putnam withheld her resignation until Dr. Elizabeth, who was living in England, could be informed of the seeming impasse. Dr. Elizabeth was tactful as ever. Dr. Putnam not only stayed on but filled the chair of *materia medica* and therapeutics for nearly twenty years.

In 1871 Dr. Putnam was standing for membership in the New York County Medical Society. Dr. Abraham Jacobi, the president, was an eminent German-born pediatrician and teacher who had settled in New York in 1853. In his official welcome to new members on December 4, 1871, Dr. Jacobi had this to say:

> It is not a small satisfaction to me that in this year of my presidency one of the most urgent questions of the day should have been quietly and noiselessly answered. The admission of females into the ranks of the medical profession—or rather (as their obtaining the degree of M.D. is a matter belonging to chartering Legislatures, and their obtaining a practice depends on the choice or prejudice of the public), into the existing

medical societies—has been decided by you by a simple vote, not attended by either hisses and clamors of excited young men in medical schools, or the confusion and derogations of the meetings of a medical association. I think we can say that our action has finally settled a question the importance of which was recognized by everybody. The vote of the largest society of this kind in the Empire State and, I believe, in the Union, will have the effect of soothing the passions and levelling prejudices in the circles of the army of medical men, forty thousand strong, in the United States, and of raising us in this respect to the standard of European countries. . . . Paris has turned out a woman doctor of medicine, who will prove, I hope, none of the least ornaments of this Society, the profession of this city, and our common country.[7]

Dr. Putnam and Dr. Jacobi met less formally when she presented an interesting heart case at a meeting of the New York Pathological Society. Dr. Jacobi asked a lot of searching questions and insisted on escorting her home so they they might continue the discussion. Taking Dr. Putnam home from medical meetings developed into a habit. They were married July 27, 1873.

Dr. Jacobi was delighted that his wife was also a talented writer and editor. He was at work on *Infant Diet*, perhaps the most famous of his several books, and Mary was of invaluable help.

After her marriage, Mary kept up with her growing practice, delivered five lectures a week at the Woman's Medical College, and helped her husband establish a pediatric clinic at Mount Sinai Hospital. Somehow she found time to do her own writing, and in 1875 she submitted a paper for The Boylston Medical Prize, a highly coveted honor granted by Harvard and one which, it was established, would never be granted to a woman. However, entries were submitted anonymously so that the judges should not be influenced by the identities of the authors. While not so intended, this provision made it possible for a woman to submit a paper. When her paper was found markedly superior to all other entries and her identity was revealed, the judges faced a dilemma. They broke with tradition and awarded her the prize.

The years following were busy ones. In 1880 she was admitted to membership in the New York Academy of Medicine. In 1882 she was appointed lecturer on children's diseases at the newly founded Post-Graduate Medical School of New York, where she taught male graduate students. She continued to be active until the middle 1890s, when her health began to deteriorate. She died in 1906.

At a memorial meeting at the Academy of Medicine on January 4, 1907, Sir William Osler, the eminent teacher, author, and champion of public health, said:

> When Mary Putnam returned from Europe with a Paris medical degree and a training in scientific medicine unusual at that date even among men, the status of women as doctors was still unsettled. . . .
>
> It is no disparagement to her contemporaries to say that no other woman in the profession equalled her in the ability with which she presented a subject. The scientific character of her numerous contributions gave a new distinction to the work of women physicians in this country, and contributed not a little to allay that strong animus which for so long kept them out of schools and medical societies. That almost everywhere the door is now open is due largely to her influence exerted unconsciously in this way. With such a training and with so keen a mind it is a great regret that the conditions here were not such as to allow her to follow a scientific career.
>
> For years I have been awaiting the advent of the modern Trotula, a woman in the profession with an intellect so commanding that she will take rank with the Harveys, the Hunters, the Pasteurs, the Virchows, and the Listers. That she has not arisen is no reflection on the small band of women who have joined our ranks in the past fifty years. Stars of the first

magnitude are rare, but that such a one will arise among women physicians I have not the slightest doubt.

And let us be thankful that when she comes she will not have to waste her precious energies in the worry of a struggle for recognition. She will be of the type of mind and training of Mary Putnam Jacobi; her victory will be not on the practical but on the scientific side, in which many new avenues are open to women. . . .

To this Felix Adler, founder of the Ethical Culture Movement, added:

Her intellectual life was keen, her intellectual interests were varied, and yet the humane interest remained supreme. This manifested itself in her tender sympathy for suffering, in her active response to every good cause, and especially in her extreme readiness to extend help and advice to the younger members of her profession, and in the high standard she held up to those who looked up to her for guidance.[8]

At the age of ten Mary Corinna Putnam had written to her grandmother: "I would do deeds, so that after I have passed into that world, that region beyond the grave, I should be spoken of with affection, so that I should live again in the hearts of those I have left behind me."[9] She did not fail this early dream.

11. Emily Dunning Barringer

Emily Dunning (1876–1961) was born in Scarsdale, New York, to secure and prosperous parents who pampered their children. But by the time Emily was eight the family had fallen on hard times. Of this circumstance she would write almost seventy years later: "Children, fortunately for the most part, do not have an awareness of change or disaster, particularly well-cared-for children. But the change did occur. . . . Actually, it was the turning point in my life not fully appreciated or realized for years after. The task of retrieving something from the wreckage of our fortune kept my father much abroad and it became for a while my mother's tragic job to take over the immediate care and support of herself and five children with another child expected at any moment."[1]

The Dunnings moved to a house they owned near Gramercy Park in New York City. Mrs. Dunning met her immediate problem by taking in paying guests. Emily, the second child and oldest girl, divided her time among school, working in the house, and taking care of two young brothers, Harry and the newborn Ned.

In 1894, Emily and her mother heard Mary Putnam Jacobi speak on education for women:

> Education is the one certain way of raising the position of women from that which it is now—dependency upon men, submission to men—in many cases, chattel slavery to men. A woman cannot demand rights if she is not qualified for them.

129

She cannot vote if she does not understand politics. She cannot teach unless she has been taught. She cannot become a lawyer, a businesswoman, a doctor, unless she has had training to fit her for these positions.

We have all heard it said that education—too much of it—makes a woman unfit to be a good wife or mother. She loses her femininity. I am not the only woman who has proved by example that this is not true. . . .

Men cannot always guarantee security to the families, no matter how much they try, and so wives—untrained, unskilled—must go to work at whatever they can to help support the family.

And what of unmarried women? . . . You know as well as I do the fate of the unmarried. As a spinster daughter or sister-in-law, she is tolerated in someone else's home to be everyone's drudge. Or she has to take in sewing, millinery or work in a shop. The wages are miserable and she is looked down upon by everyone. . . .[2]

Dr. Mary Jacobi then spoke of the very few men's colleges that admitted women and of the existing women's colleges struggling to raise their standards.

The speech made a deep impression on Mrs. Dunning. A practical woman, she knew that a girl with no dowry was unlikely to make a good match, if she caught a husband at all. On the other hand, she hesitated to make the decision that would commit her daughter to a world of men not yet ready to grant professional status to women. Her mind was made up for her when a well-meaning friend proposed that Emily be apprenticed to a milliner. Emily had a "gift" for hat-making and had, in addition to her other chores, become milliner for the family that could no longer afford to buy hats.

On her friend's departure, Mrs. Dunning called Emily into the room. Emily later recalled: "I found her with her back pressed tight against the door, her face . . . gray and drawn, tired; her hands out flat by her side pressing backward with the tendons and veins taut. 'Emily,' she said, 'you are going to go to college.' " [3]

EDUCATION

The Dunning girls and the Jacobis' daughter, Marjorie, attended the same school, and it was easy for Emily and her mother to consult Dr. Mary Jacobi about Emily's college career. When Emily proposed a career in nursing, Dr. Mary Jacobi said: "You are only a child. You are too young to know what you really want to do. Get ready and go to college and get a good scientific training, and I will predict that when you graduate you will go on into the study of medicine rather than nursing."[4] She recommended Cornell University at Ithaca, New York, where Dr. Burt G. Wilder and Professor Simon P. Gage were working out what she considered to be the best, possibly the only, medical preparatory course in the country.

In September 1894 eighteen-year-old Emily Dunning entered Cornell. Her tuition was paid by her uncle, Henry Sage (who, with Andrew D. White and Ezra Cornell, was one of the founders of Cornell). Her family gave her what support they could. It was not long before Dr. Mary Jacobi's prediction was realized. "I had been in Cornell University only a short time," wrote Emily, "when all doubts vanished as to whether I should go into nursing or medicine. I knew irrevocably that I would choose medicine as my life work."[5]

The lot of a woman student in the nineties could be a far from happy one. Emily's was different. She met male students' expressions of contempt and their assumption that the female brain was inferior with a friendly frankness and a challenge that suggested she would prove herself their equal. She invariably did. In fact, she so outstripped her fellows that she completed the Cornell four-year course in three years—no easy feat. The next step was the Woman's Medical College of the New York Infirmary for Women and Children, then the Cornell University Medical College, when students of the Women's school were transferred to it in 1898.

The new college was directly across from Bellevue Hospital, whose beginnings dated back to the days when New York City was still New Amsterdam. By the end of the nineteenth century it had become one of America's largest hospitals. Bedside instruction was given the Cornell students at Bellevue.

The pace was hectic. Emily had little time for her fellow students until one day Benjamin Stockwell Barringer introduced himself. It did not take them long to discover that they were well suited to each other, but marriage was out of the question. Neither had finished medical school, and that has to be followed by a two-year internship.

THE SEARCH FOR AN INTERNSHIP

In 1901 a woman with a medical degree could intern at a women's hospital, a post easily obtainable, or fight for a place at one of the "regular" hospitals that mostly excluded women. If she gambled on a regular hospital and lost, internships at women's hospitals would then be filled. She would have the title of doctor but no place to function as one.

Once again, Emily consulted Mary Putnam Jacobi. The latter, a fighter for hospital opportunities for women physicians, told her to enter the fight. "Women must be willing to go up, to be knocked down again and again, before the general hospitals will finally be opened," she said. When Emily asked what would happen to her if she failed to gain a place, as she almost certainly would, Dr. Mary Jacobi was quick to promise, "If that happens, I will take you into my office as my assistant until your plans are made."[6]

The road to the stiff competitive examinations for internships in the coveted "big hospitals" involved extracurricular studies. These were covered by the "Hospital Quiz," conducted by Dr. John Rogers. The quiz had never been open to women. Emily, however, seems to have had little difficulty in persuading Dr. Rogers to let her participate.

Emily applied to five hospitals, all of which refused to consider her on the grounds of lack of precedent. Then Dr. Mary Jacobi suggested Mount Sinai, where a woman gynecologist had been permitted to serve on the staff some years earlier. Permission to take the reputedly stiff examination seemed reasonably assured when the personal backing of Dr. Mary Jacobi produced favorable reactions from a few influential members of the board of trustees. That was not enough. The trustees stated that they would not appoint a woman to the staff even if she should win a place. Recalling Dr. Jacobi's words, "Women must be willing to go up, to be knocked down again and again," Emily decided to sit for the examination anyway.

She had been warned that she would not be told her rating, and it was not until 1939, when she was sixty-three, that she learned how she had done. Then the New York City Commissioner of Hospitals, Sigmund S. Goldwater, told Dr. Emily Dunning Barringer that he owed his start in life to her. She asked what he meant. "Do you remember that examination at Mount Sinai?" he inquired. "Well, I took it with you; you won first place, but because you could not have it, it was awarded to me."[7]

By now most of the hospitals had completed their examinations. The few that still had openings did not have facilities for women interns. Bellevue was a prime example. Since it was here that many women medical students received bedside training, it would have been the logical place for them to intern, but Bellevue interns were housed in dormitories.

Then Emily learned that Gouverneur Hospital had a room in which she might sleep. Gouverneur, a branch of Bellevue, was an emergency hospital in the most densely populated part of the city. She lost no time making the rounds of the medical board of the hospital. The objections members raised were typical—Miss Dunning could not possibly work with the drunks and addicts that were the hospital's chief customers; she would not be able to tolerate their obscene language; the nurses would resent working under a woman doctor; the peace of mind of male doctors would be upset by the presence of a woman on the staff and their work would suffer accordingly. The board, however, prompted by Dr. John Rogers (who predicted that the staff would either fall in love with her or hate her), Dr. John F. Erdman, and Dr. Louis J. Ladin, "did not seem too apprehensive in regard to the proposition I laid before them. . . ."[8] The members agreed to permit her to take the competitive examination, undertaking to appoint her if she qualified. The published results showed that she had placed first. She and the three men who had placed second, third, and fourth would fill the vacancies at Gouverneur.

Yet another obstacle blocked her way. Gouverneur was a city hospital. Appointments had to be ratified by the City Commissioner, John W. Keller. He announced emphatically: "I will not be responsible for having a young woman doctor out on that ambulance and have her break her neck."[9] There was no appeal.

During the next year, while Emily Dunning was working for Dr. Mary Jacobi, advocates of civil and social reform were bringing pressure to bear on reform mayor Seth Low. The Reverend Percy Stickney Grant, rector of the Church of the Ascension on lower Fifth Avenue, a supporter of women's rights, asked Emily to prepare a statement to be forwarded to the mayor. Her statement stressed the advantages to the community to be gained by admitting women to hospital staffs and also the advantages to the individual women physicians.

In the spring of 1902 the mayor announced that the competitive examination at Gouverneur Hospital would be open to women and that if a woman won a place it would be given her. There was one stipulation: the appointment was to be accepted on the same terms offered to men, which meant a two-year internship—one year in general medicine and one in general surgery—and a year and a half on ambulance duty.

Now that the battle was won, Emily was reluctant to compete. Many changes had taken place in medicine and surgery in the year since she had last taken the examination. Medical journals were full of new theories and techniques. Textbooks had been revised. Medical students had kept up; Emily had not. When she pointed out to Dr. Mary Jacobi that there were some excellent women in the Cornell senior class, the doctor was unyielding. Emily went to work.

It was tough going all the way, and her examination performance fell short of that of the previous year when she had placed first. In fact, her written answers were not good enough to ensure her appearance before the examiners for the oral clinical examination. She became eligible only when there was a last-minute increase in the number of interns to be appointed. At the oral examination her confidence returned. With a year of practical experience to back her up, answers came easily. It seems certain that, if her written responses had been better, the examiners would again have put her in first place. As it was she rated fourth.

Emily would not start work at Gouverneur until January 1903. For the first time in her life she had a chance to take a vacation—to see something of her family and her friends, and of Ben Barringer. She undertook to assist Dr. Mary Jacobi when needed, but not to work for her regularly as she had during the previous year.

INTERNSHIP

When Dr. Dunning reported for work the four interns who were her immediate superiors and who definitely did not want her at Gouverneur did their utmost to embarrass her. She was assigned tasks that patients considered immodest for a woman to undertake. Emily met these attempts to drive her out of the hospital calmly and efficiently, and her work on the wards and in the dispensary gained her the respect and gratitude of patients. By her own account her persecutors "were to stage a royal battle, but they did not recognize that our referees would be the patients and nurses, the hospital authorities, the ambulance drivers, the press, the police and the citizens of the East Side. I was loth to enter this struggle with my professional brothers. I accepted their challenge because I had to."[10]

There was no decrease in the harassment during her first six months. Her tormentors repeatedly talked in front of her of the dangers involved in ambulance service. They spoke of the physical strength needed to hang on when the ambulance was highballing through the streets and of the times each had come close to falling off. They described the places to which calls took them—saloons, dens of vice, filthy alleys—to pick up victims of every conceivable crime, including murder attempts. They discussed opium addicts and drunks who had no respect for a doctor's uniform. Since Gouverneur was an emergency hospital, patients requiring protracted hospitalization were transferred by horse-drawn ambulance to Bellevue. The ambulance also shuttled the sick between their homes or the streets and the hospital or careened to an accident or a fire behind madly racing horses. Emily was ready to take the risk of breaking her neck in the performance of ambulance service, but where was she to find clothes suitable for jumping up and down from the ambulance? A long, full skirt would be hampering and might trip her; a short, tight one would be considered immodest. Her uniform must have plenty of pockets but must not be mannish. She put the matter in the hands of V. Ballard and Sons of Boston, a firm from whom she had ordered a habit when she took up riding. The uniform settled upon was a two-piece affair. The jacket of navy blue serge lined with satin was tight-waisted and military in appearance. The skirt, which came to the ankles, was narrow enough for movement and wide enough for modesty. Pockets were cleverly hidden in all parts of the uniform. There was a mackintosh to be worn over it to keep out winter cold and rain. High-laced black calfskin shoes would serve in fair weather, galoshes that buckled halfway up to the knee in foul.

Dr. Dunning's first ambulance call came early on the evening of June 30. A patient was to be transferred from Beth Israel Hospital to Bellevue.

The ambulance of the day was so designed that, unless the doctor was in the narrow boxlike interior taking care of the patient, he was required to perch on an exposed slippery seat, actually more a ledge than a seat, at the back of the vehicle. The ambulance driver, Dick Bateman, friendly and sympathetic, devised a method by which she could safely and swiftly mount to her place. It involved stepping up, seating herself, swinging her skirt and feet over the tailboard, whirling herself around to face forward, and reaching with both hands for the leather straps—all in one movement!

The trip from Gouverneur to Beth Israel to Bellevue and back took them through poor districts on New York's Lower East Side. The crowds in the hot streets gaped at the woman on the back step. Their comments were crude. She took it all in good part. Mission accomplished, she returned to the hospital with a feeling of exhilaration.

Early next morning Dr. Dunning was back on the ambulance for what was to be a long, hard day. Her driver was Tom White. He proved as friendly as Dick Bateman. What was even more valuable to the fledgling ambulance surgeon was the fact that White's long experience had turned him into something of a diagnostician. He could tell whether an unconscious man was a potential patient or just another drunk. "All day long," Emily wrote, "he would whisper, 'Take him in, Doc' or 'He is all right, take him to the Police Station.' There all drunks were removed for a sobering period."[11] The third driver, Tom Murray, was equally anxious to get her started right.

The calls covered a variety of situations. If no emergency was involved, the progress could be a pleasant one—like a Sunday afternoon drive. If it was an emergency, the ambulance went at a clip that made her wonder if she could keep her grip on the leather straps.

One memorable call took her to the waterfront. The policeman who had put in the call was shocked when he found himself faced by a woman. After all, it was necessary for the doctor to climb down into the ship's hold. Despite the doctor's assurances that she could manage, he insisted that they be accompanied by another policeman so that she would be protected from above and below as they went hand over hand down a rope ladder. She treated the broken bones in the sailor's feet and watched while he was hoisted aloft. Then without hesitation she returned up the rope ladder. "I learned very early," she later wrote of this incident, "to obey always the orders of the police, and when they told me to do a certain thing, I went ahead and did it without question. There were many occasions when it was fortunate for me that I responded in this way to their lead. In this case had I hesitated and looked down into the dizzy depths of the hold, I might easily have become panic stricken."[12]

The senior surgeon was one of the four staff members determined to break Emily's spirit. He worked her unmercifully. There were ambulance calls day and night interspersed with work in the accident ward on patients she brought in, surgery duty, and everything else he could think up. Overworked, Emily was fearful of making mistakes. And she was often lonely. In face of the continuing harassment by the seniors, the junior interns did not dare to take her part or even be friendly. The best they could do for her was to remain neutral. She did have allies in the ambulance drivers, the policemen, who came to respect her, the patients she helped and the East Side poor whom they told of her help, and even some of the nurses.

The summer passed. Winter came, bringing rain and sleet, driving winds, snowstorms, blizzards, and treacherous ice. Winter was on the side of the doctors who were trying to dislodge her. Although from January 1904 on Dr. Dunning had enough seniority not to be on first ambulance call, they kept her at it. The suffering was worthwhile. She was learning things that she could never have hoped to learn elsewhere. At the end of June the last of her tormentors departed, and she stepped officially into the role of house surgeon. From October until mid-December, when she completed her training at Gouverneur, she served as chief resident. The evening after her departure from Gouverneur, a delegation of ambulance drivers, policemen, politicians, settlement workers, and ordinary citizens of the Lower East Side appeared at the Dunning home to present her with the following expression of their appreciation:

TESTIMONIAL

from the

Citizens of New York,

the Police of the 7th, 12th, and 13th precincts,

and the Ambulance Drivers of Gouverneur Hospital

to

DR. EMILY DUNNING

upon her retirement, January 1, 1905, as

Chief of Staff of Gouverneur Hospital, New York

Dr. Dunning

for two years served the hospital and the people of New York in a manner that has won the admiration and esteem of her fellow-workers and all those with whom she has been brought in contact. Her wonderful skill, conscientious and untiring efforts, charm of manner, devotion to her patients, extreme kindness and consideration for all who labored with her, have endeared her to all.

AS THE ONLY WOMAN AMBULANCE SURGEON
IN THE WORLD

she has won distinction that is world-wide and brought honor, not only upon herself but upon her sex, her profession, Gouverneur Hospital and the City of New York.

We hope and pray that the future may hold happiness and additional honors in store for her, and *Our best wishes* follow her in her new labors.[13]

Benjamin Barringer and Emily Dunning were married the following Saturday at eight in the morning. At ten they sailed for Europe, where both were to study in Vienna.

Dr. Emily Dunning Barringer went on to fight for the cause of women in medicine. Her efforts were rewarded when in April 1943 the United States Senate sent to the White House for signature a bill commissioning women physicians and surgeons in the medical corps of the army and navy.

12. Alice Hamilton

The records show that Alice Hamilton (1869–1970) was born in New York City, but her true home, to which she was brought at the age of six weeks, was in Indiana. Her father's father had emigrated from northern Ireland to Fort Wayne as a young man and was later joined there by his father. Hers was the fourth generation to live in what they called "the Old House." It is understandable, therefore, that much of Dr. Hamilton's pioneer work in medicine would center on the Midwest.

Alice's parents, Montgomery Hamilton and Gertrude Pond Hamilton, believed that girls were as much entitled to an education as boys were, and they had their own ideas about what that education should include. Alice later recalled: "We had a smattering of mathematics, taught by a day governess, but I never got beyond the beginnings of algebra. We learned what our parents thought important: languages, literature, history. We had formal training only in languages; the other subjects we had to learn by reading, and we did. . . . The habit of doing one's own searching for the knowledge we wanted was valuable."[1]

Miss Porter's School in Farmington, Connecticut, was traditional for Hamilton girls. As each reached the age of seventeen, she was sent there for two years. In all, ten Miss Hamiltons attended, the last being Alice's youngest sister.

When Alice returned to Fort Wayne in 1888, it was evident that the fortunes of the pioneering Hamilton family were in decline. If the girls were to have a meaningful life they would have to work. Careers then open to women of their station in life were limited to teaching, nursing, and, despite its difficulty, the practice of medicine. Alice chose medicine, she later wrote, "not because I was scientifically-minded, for I was deeply ignorant of science. I chose it because as a doctor I could go anywhere I pleased—to far-off lands or to city slums—and could be quite sure that I could be of use anywhere."[2]

Alice spent a year studying physics and chemistry with a high-school teacher and anatomy at a third-rate medical school in Fort Wayne. She went on to the medical school of the University of Michigan at Ann Arbor, from which she graduated in 1893. It was her intention to enter the new field of pathology, which is the study of changes in body tissue caused by disease and the reactions of such tissue to disease. However, George Dock (1860–1951), her professor of medicine (who in 1896 would describe the first case of coronary occlusion in America proved by autopsy), persuaded her to take some hospital training first. He maintained that otherwise her knowledge and experience would be too one-sided. She therefore devoted a year to interning in Boston before going on to Germany, where, reputedly, the best work in pathology and bacteriology was being done. After studying in Leipzig and Munich, she came to the conclusion that "in bacteriology Leipzig had nothing to give me that I had not already had [at Ann Arbor] . . . but neither Germans nor Americans would have believed it."[3]

Back in America in 1896, Alice found that American doctors were as yet paying little attention to the pathologist and his work. Her year in Germany had in a sense been wasted. Nobody wanted pathologist Hamilton. With no job in sight she decided to devote the winter to studying pathological anatomy under Simon Flexner at the Johns Hopkins Medical School.

The following summer she received and accepted an offer to teach pathology in the Northwestern University Woman's Medical School in Chicago, a post she would hold until 1902. But she felt that she would never be more than a fourth-rate bacteriologist and decided to devote herself to problems of direct human interest. To this end she began spending as much time as she could spare from teaching working at Hull-House, which had been established by Jane Addams in 1889. Alice Hamilton went to live at Hull-House in 1897.

A NEW SPECIALTY

Hull-House residents lived as neighbors of the city's poor, which included bewildered and exploited immigrants. Dr. Hamilton heard gruesome tales of accidents and illnesses suffered by factory workers. The illnesses included carbon monoxide poisoning in the steel mills, lead palsy among painters, pneumonia and rheumatism at the stockyards.

There were at this time no baby clinics in Chicago. Miss Addams allowed Dr. Hamilton to set up a baby clinic in the shower-bath room in the basement of the gymnasium. (". . . Though I did not feel at all competent to treat sick babies," wrote Alice, "I did venture to open a well-baby clinic. . . ."[4]) Contact with the mothers of the babies confirmed much of what she had heard of the disregard for human life and the suffering prevalent in industry.

Industrial medicine was a recognized medical discipline in Germany, Britain, Austria, Holland, Scandinavia, and even Italy and Spain, but not in the United States. The better-paid American industrial worker, it was argued, did not suffer the evils to which the European worker with his much lower standard of living was subjected. When she "talked to . . . medical friends about the strange silence on this subject in American medical magazines and textbooks, [she] gained the impression that here was a subject tainted with Socialism or with female sentimentality for the poor. The American Medical Association had never had a meeting devoted to this subject, and except for a few surgeons attached to large companies operating steel mills, or railways, or coal mines, there were no medical men in Illinois who specialized in the field of industrial medicine."[5]

One of the few rebels against the conspiracy of silence that blanketed working conditions was Professor Charles R. Henderson (1848–1915), chairman of the Sociology Department of the University of Chicago. He had studied and found admirable the German system of insurance for the working classes and was anxious to see it introduced into America. In 1910 he was able to persuade the governor of Illinois to appoint an Occupational Disease Commission to make the first survey of industrial sickness to be undertaken by any state. Dr. Henderson had Dr. Hamilton appointed to the commission. Her assignment: to determine the causes of plumbism, or lead poisoning.

It was common belief that lead poisoning was caused by the handling of food with unwashed hands. Therefore the only rule established by management for the protection of the workers was that they carefully wash their hands before going home. A worker who became ill was accused of not complying with this regulation.

Dr. Hamilton was convinced from the start that plumbism resulted from the inhalation of lead dust and lead fumes. She proposed to track down cases of plumbism with a view to convincing management that the problem was a serious one. The difficulty was locating victims or evidence of their disease. Workers who became ill simply dropped out of sight—illness was the price they expected to pay for being poor. Since labor was cheap and plentiful no one went looking for workers. A foreman rarely knew the last names of the men who worked under him. Nor did the company keep records of employees' names and addresses. Hospital records proved of limited help. The typical intern did not recognize plumbism when he saw it. He was apt to attribute the patient's illness to the effects of drinking too much.

After months of unrelenting search through Chicago's Serbian, Bulgarian, and Polish quarters, Dr. Hamilton was able to document twenty-two cases of plumbism from lead and dust fumes. When she presented her findings to Edward Cornish of Chicago's National Lead Company, he was not slow to act. An adequate ventilating system was installed. Men in close contact with dry lead were equipped with specially designed respirators. A medical department was established, and each worker was examined weekly by a doctor. Other factories followed National's lead.

In 1911 the State of Illinois passed a law providing for compensation for industrial diseases caused by poisonous fumes, gases, or dusts.

In the meantime Dr. Hamilton had attended the International Congress of Occupational Accidents and Diseases held in Brussels in September 1910. Here she met Charles O'Neill, Commissioner of Labor in the United States Department of Commerce. Of the Congress and this meeting Dr. Hamilton wrote later: "This was an important journey for me, not only because it taught me much in the field of preventive hygiene but even more because it resulted in a definite break away from laboratory research and the taking up of this new specialty as my life's work."[6]

The commissioner suggested she make a nationwide study similar to the one she had undertaken in Chicago. Extending her investigations beyond lead poisoning, she visited mines, quarries, factories, mills, and construction sites. She found stonecutters with "dead fingers"—hands numb and gray from the vibrations of air hammers. She found quarry workers with tuberculosis and sand blasters with silicosis, both caused by the constant inhaling of rock dust. She found that benzol, a highly dangerous chemical then used in shoe and rubber factories, attacked the bone marrow, which produces the blood cells in the body. The result was anemia and severe bleeding under the skin and from the gums and nose. She found that tunnel workers were subject to "caisson disease"; the men suffered severe damage to the brain and spinal cord as a result of being moved rapidly and directly from the compression chambers in which they worked to normal atmosphere. The symptoms were violent pain in the limbs ("the bends") and brain disturbances ("the blind staggers"). This problem was solved by the introduction of a series of decompression chambers. In the last study she did (1937–38), she found that the carbon disulfide used in processing viscose rayon (an early synthetic fiber) caused paralysis and insanity.

Besides the illnesses there were frequent injuries, including the accidental severance of fingers and limbs and even the loss of sight. These occurred because safety regulations were few and seldom observed. Year after year she submitted reports to Washington on the appalling conditions in American industry. She lectured and wrote books and magazine articles. Reforms came slowly, but they did come.

OTHER CAUSES

Alice Hamilton espoused causes that were, to say the least, ahead of their time. In the early 1900s she was already advocating birth control, and in 1915 she was involved in pacifist activities. She attended an international congress of women at The Hague in Holland, whose objective was to bring an end to the war then raging in Europe by having delegations of neutral women visit the capitals of the warring nations in an attempt at mediation. The undertaking failed, and the participants were dubbed pacifists, often with derogatory implications.

In late 1918, shortly after Dr. Hamilton had delivered the Cutter lectures at the Harvard Medical School (a recognized prelude to faculty appointment), she and Miss Addams attended a meeting of the Women's International League for Permanent Peace. They were asked by the Quakers of America to look into the condition of children in defeated Germany while they were abroad.

Dr. Hamilton was appalled. "My German diary is a succession of pictures of starvation, as seen in the crèches and kindergartens and schools, in hospitals and sanatoria for the tuberculous, and in outdoor camps for boys and girls. I saw then face to face what I had never seen before except in the illustrations of medical books—extreme cases of marasmus (a wasting away of body tissues caused by malnutrition). . . . All were naked [at the outdoor camps] for they must get sunshine on their bodies, to make up in part for the lack of fats, so we could see plainly the little sticklike legs, the swollen bellies, the ribs one could count, the shoulder blades sticking out like wings. And we saw them eat their midday meal, a bowl of 'soup'— hot water with coarsely ground grains, chopped green leaves, and a few drops of margarine."[7] She and Miss Addams returned home resolved to do what they could to soften the postwar feeling toward conquered Germany and to raise funds for the feeding centers the Quakers were planning to open.

With eyebrows already raised at her pacifist connections, Dr. Hamilton was now accused of being pro-German. A generous contributor to the medical school advised a member of the Harvard Corporation that she would never give another penny if someone who went about rousing people's sympathies for Germany was on the faculty. Dr. Hamilton was asked to refute the charge but refused to do so. She stated that she would continue to speak as often as she could on the subject of the starving German children and to raise money for them. The contributor's protest was firmly quashed by Dean David Edsall of the medical school, and Dr. Hamilton became assistant professor of industrial medicine. She also taught preventive medicine and public health. In 1935 she retired from Harvard as Professor Emeritus of Industrial Medicine.

The health of people everywhere was a concern to her. Appointed a member of the Health Committee of the League of Nations in 1924, she studied health problems all over Europe.

Alice Hamilton lived to be a hundred and one. She was often ahead of her time, never behind it. At the age of eighty she said to S. J. Woolf, an artist-reporter who was writing an article about her for *The New York Times Magazine,* "If you are going to sketch me, I'll take off my hat, for nothing dates one so much as a hat, and I refuse to be dated."[8]

Surely her own epitaph!

PART THREE

Women in Related Fields

13. Nursing— from Nuns to Nightingale

Nursing is one of the world's oldest arts. In its earliest days nursing was often indistinguishable from the practice of medicine and surgery. This was particularly true in those primitive societies in which sickness was the province of medicine women rather than medicine men. On the other hand, where there were medicine men, they were frequently served by persons of lesser status, often women, who carried out their therapeutic instructions, dressed wounds, and so on. These helpers may properly be regarded as the first nurses.

Early medical records that have survived rarely mention nursing. This is hardly surprising. As the historian of nursing Minnie Goodnow has pointed out, "men do not make records of ordinary events, but only the unusual or striking ones. People nursed their sick as a matter of course."[1]

The functions and qualifications of the nurse were defined as early as the fourth century B.C. Charaka, a distinguished Hindu physician, wrote in his Compendium:

> The Physician, the Drugs, the Nurse, and the Patient constitute an aggregate of four. Of what virtue each of these should be possessed, so as to become causes for the cure of disease, should be known. . . .
>
> Nurse—Knowledge of the manner in which drugs should be prepared or compounded for administration, cleverness, devo-

tion to the patient waited upon, and purity (both of mind and body) are the four qualifications of the attending nurse.[2]

A similar definition has survived from Ceylon:

> The nurse must be clever, devoted to the patient, and pure in body and mind; must know how to compound drugs, be competent to cook food, skilled in bathing the patients, conversant with rubbing the limbs and massage, with lifting the patient and assisting him to walk about, well skilled in making and cleaning of beds, ready, patient, and skilful, never unwilling to do anything that is ordered.[3]

King Asoka (c. 225 B.C.) of Ceylon built eighteen hospitals in which the attendants were men and evidently called nurses. One of his predecessors, King Parackramabahoo, who appears to have lived prior to 500 B.C., built "great hospitals for the use of the sick people, furnishing them with victuals, and slave boys and maidens to wait upon and nourish the sick."[4] The ancient Persians also had houses for the sick poor who were waited on by slave boys and girls.

The temple of Aesculapius at Epidauros included a hospital ward, and the priestesses who were among those serving in it may or may not have been nurses.

Hippocrates speaks of the assistant as a co-worker of the physician. He makes no direct reference to nurses and their work, but it is clear that the women of Greece worked as nurses, since the mistress of the household was charged with nursing sick slaves. Slaves were, of course, very valuable property.

The Roman soldier, mainstay of the empire, was given the best nursing care available. At first this service was performed in private houses; later the sick and wounded were cared for in tents or separate buildings by women and old men. Still later there were military hospitals with a class of orderlies *(nosocomi)* serving as nurses.

In the early days of Christianity the new church introduced half a dozen orders for women. Deaconesses, widows, and nuns were especially concerned with nursing. The deaconess was ordained by the bishop to perform the same functions as her male counterpart. The first was Phebe (A.D. 60), of whom St. Paul said: "She hath been a succourer of many and of myself also" (Romans 16:3).[5]

The order of deaconesses must be regarded as the forerunner of visiting nurse associations, since they cared for the sick in their homes as well as in hospitals. They were active in Syria, Asia Minor, all of Italy, and even in Spain, Gaul, and Ireland. In the year 400 there were forty deaconesses functioning as parish nurses in Constantinople. While the order remained active in the Eastern Church until the eighth century, its days as a functioning religious order were numbered. In the fifth and sixth centuries Gallic councils deprived the order of its clerical character. Then, when the Synod of Orleans forbade the ordaining of women in 533, the order was in effect abolished.

Nursing sisterhoods made their appearance around the year 500. At first its members were bound by no vows and adopted no distinctive dress. As the clergy assumed authority, vows and a distinctive habit became customary.

The oldest purely nursing order in the world was that of the Augustinian Sisters, who served the Hôtel Dieu in Paris, which was founded by Bishop Landry in 1605. M. Adelaide Nutting and Lavinia L. Dock, who wrote their history of nursing in the early 1900s, have given us a graphic picture of them.

For twelve centuries, they wrote, generations of Augustinian Sisters toiled "in complete self-abnegation and renunciation even through their old age, often to die in harness like poor old wornout patient horses. And from the thirteenth century on, at least, if not before, their lot seems to have been made needlessly bare and hard. Not only was their work almost cruelly heavy, but they were denied that light of knowledge and of understanding which does so much to brighten the severest toil. They were cut off from all share in the intellectual life, and even the course of outer human progress was closed to them. For them professional instruction did not exist. Only a routine handed down from one to another approached anything

that could be called teaching. What wonder that in time they atro-
phied mentally and became incapable of progress; that science left
them behind and that a changed environment found them unable to
adapt themselves to it?"⁶

In the sixth century Sacerdos, archbishop of Lyon, was responsible for the establishment of an Hôtel Dieu in his city. He persuaded
Childebert I, king of the Franks, to erect what was to become one
of the largest and most complete hospitals in all of France. The
nurses that staffed the Lyon hospital were not members of a religious
order. They were *servantes chambrières, filles repenties,* and *péni-
tentes*—in short, prostitutes who wished to lead a better life. Many
of them were patients of the hospital who subsequently dedicated
themselves to its service. Thirtèen and a half centuries later, Dr.
Anna Hamilton told the Third International Congress of Nurses at
Buffalo, New York, that their successors "are given an elementary
professional education in the hospital, are fairly well disciplined, and
are free to leave the service and to marry. . . . But, free and liberal
as their constitution is, they receive no real training in the modern
sense and their work is behind the times and crude."⁷

Unique among the early secular orders that took no vows were the
Béguines of Flanders (Belgium). There is some question as to when
the order was founded and by whom, but there is evidence to suggest
that it may have been as early as the seventh century, though the
date has been placed as late as 1234.⁸ The early Béguine women,
disgusted by the evils that had crept into monastic life, both male
and female, sought self-expression and self-denial in work beyond
the church's dictation. They formed communities in which they led
a pious life apart from men, supporting themselves by making and
selling lace. Because of its secular nature members have been free to
leave the order and marry at will. The Béguines, who are still active,
have always done both hospital and private nursing.

To think that the pendulum made a complete swing from the male
nurses of Hindu and other early civilizations to the deaconesses,
nuns, and other dedicated women of the first millennium A.D. would

be to distort the facts. Down through history, different classes of people, male and female, have provided different degrees of nursing care in different parts of the world.

THE HOSPITALLER ORDERS

In medieval times, when there existed male religious orders that included nursing among their duties, nursing must have been about equally shared between men and women. With the start of the Crusades in 1096 there was a marked resurgence of men in nursing.

The earliest reference to a hospital in Jerusalem seems to be that of Bernard, a French monk, who in 870 made his pilgrimage. He found there "an hospital for the Latins, and in the same house a library collected by the care and at the expense of Charlemagne."[9]

About 1050 some rich merchants of Amalfi (Italy) established two hospitals, one for each sex, in Jerusalem. The male hospital, under the protection of St. John the Almoner (of Cyprus) was the incubator of the famous Knights Hospitallers of St. John of Jerusalem, a fraternity that later built hospitals in Rhodes and Malta.

The knights were men of rank, some of whom fought in the Crusades and some of whom, with little or no training, served as physicians. "Half-knights," or serving brothers, men of a lower social order, did the actual nursing of the sick. The English branch of the order, founded in 1100, still maintains hospitals and does nursing.

The Crusades, which continued for almost two hundred years, brought in their wake an upsurge of Hospitaller fraternities. The best known among them, besides the Knights of St. John, were the Red Cross Knights (1119), the Teutonic Knights Hospitallers (1191), and the Knights of St. Lazarus. Some historians have attempted to trace the St. Lazarus Hospitallers back to the hospital built by St. Basil in Cesarea in 370, but generally the beginning of the order is associated with the Crusades. There were, incidentally, sisters of this order.

HOSPITALS, PUBLIC AND PRIVATE

There were few large hospitals prior to the twelfth century. As cities grew and church hospitals no longer sufficed to take care of the sick, city hospitals were built to supplement them. These were as fine architecturally as the church hospitals, but in function they fell far short of them.

The men put in charge of municipal hospitals were not physicians and they knew nothing about nursing. There was no superintendent of nurses to train and guide those who undertook nursing. With no religious motives to inspire them, the nurses grew increasingly aware of the seamy side of their work. They considered themselves servants rather than angels of mercy. Others shared their view.

People of means did not go to hospitals. They were nursed at home by members of the family, servants, and the children's "nurse," who was frequently retained by the family even after the children were grown to serve as sick nurse when needed. The hospitals were filled with common people who had no rights. They did not expect consideration and they got none. To avoid loss of time for the so-called doctors, several patients occupied the operating room at the same time. Those whose turn was yet to come had to witness the agonies of patients held down on the table by strong men.

This inhumane contempt for the patient inevitably spread to the nursing staff. No attempt was made to cure medical cases. Patients received little or no care, bedsores were commonplace, and infections spread through the hospitals like wildfire. Every hospital was a pesthouse.

By the end of the thirteenth century some effort was being made to remedy this situation. Throughout Europe thousands of hospitals were built by kings, prelates, rich merchants looking toward salvation, and good women. Women were re-entering nursing. At the beginning of the fourteenth century, two hundred thousand women were visiting the sick and treating disease in and out of hospitals.[10] Permanent orders of nursing sisters were being founded; their members were protected from harm by both church and state. The Gray Nuns of St. Francis and the Poor Clares in Italy were considered as qualified to take care of the sick as the so-called physicians.

The thirteenth-century Hospital of Santa Maria della Scala in Siena is still in operation; its nurses perform in essentially the same way as their predecessors and wear habits that have been little changed. There is a tendency to assume that hospital conditions and standards of nursing prior to the nineteenth century were always primitive, but at the Siena hospital the patients' beds were comfortable, stuffed with moss and covered with leather to keep out the moisture; a table standing at the head of each bed facilitated the feeding of patients; and a urinal was close at hand.

Mahout, countess of Artois (d. 1329), is credited with building nearly one hundred hospitals throughout France. The one near her castle at Artois boasted a large airy ward with windows at both ends. On sunny days the sick were laid on soft cushions in front of the windows. Comforts that the patients did not enjoy at home were typical of the private hospitals.

The number of hospitals built and supervised by royal patrons in the fourteenth and fifteenth centuries did not suffice. Conditions in public hospitals, such as the Hôtel Dieu in Paris, were abominable. The rich (if they were foolish enough to commit themselves) and the poor, the sick, and the dying, lay side by side on vermin-infested beds of straw. The overworked, poorly fed, frequently degraded and punished nuns, whose only reward lay in heaven, did their best. They prescribed, prepared, and administered medicines. They even washed bedclothes in the Seine. But the beds remained dirty, the walls covered with vermin. The stench in the wards was so frightful that the head nun made her rounds with a perfumed handkerchief pressed to her nose.

In England a hospital at York was built by King Athelstan around 936, believed to be England's first. It employed eight nursing sisters. St. Bartholomew's of Rochester, founded in 1080, has continued in operation without interruption.

Queen Matilda built St. Giles in the East (also known as St. Giles in the Fields) in 1101. She established an order of Poor Clares to work in its wards. About fifty years later she erected the hospital of St. Katherine as a memorial to her two children. Nursing at St. Katherine's was undertaken by women of noble birth.

London's still active St. Bartholomew's Hospital was built in 1123 by Rahere, a king's jester turned Augustinian monk. The nursing staff consisted of eight monks and four nuns.

St. Thomas's Hospital, later the site of the Nightingale School, was founded in 1213 by Richard, prior of Bermondsey.

In early days few doctors were to be found beyond the limits of major cities. Self-taught monks and nuns doctored the community. Noblewomen took care of their servants and dependents. All who were educated were taught a smattering of medicine. No distinction was made between the work of doctors and that of the nurses.

After the monasteries were suppressed in the early sixteenth century, church hospitals were taken over by the cities in which they were located. Much of what is today the province of nursing was performed by doctors and medical students. Nurses did little more for the patients than bathe them, supervise their bodily functions, make their beds, and serve their meals; the rest of their time was given over to such menial tasks as scrubbing the floors and washing dishes.

Everywhere the nursing art continued to deteriorate and by the middle of the nineteenth century had sunk "to an indescribable level of degradation. . . . Solely among the religious orders did nursing remain an interest and some remnants of technique survive." In England, after the suppression of the religious orders practically no nursing class remained. "It was forgotten that a refined woman could be a nurse, except perhaps in her own family."[11]

Nurses were so ill fed, overworked, and ill treated that no one would take the job if she could get anything else to do. The following hospital rules, published in 1789, clearly reflect the caliber of those who pretended to take care of patients:

No dirt, rags, or bones may be thrown from the windows.

Nurses are to punctually shift the bed and body linen of the patients, viz., their sheets once in a fortnight, their shirts once in four days, their drawers and stockings once a week or oftener if found necessary.

All nurses who disobey orders, get drunk, neglect their patients, quarrel or fight with other nurses, or quarrel with men, shall be immediately discharged.[12]

One hospital superintendent said, "If I can but obtain a set of nurses who are sober, it is as much as I can hope for."[13]

Not until 1825 was there any attempt to raise the quality of nursing. That year Dr. Robert Gooch proposed to the Methodists and the Quakers the establishment of "an order of women, selected for their good sense, industry, kindliness and piety, [to] be placed as pupil nurses in the hospitals of Edinburgh and London."[14]

In 1849 Elizabeth Fry (of prison-reform fame) was persuaded by Dr. Gooch and poet laureate Robert Southey to form the Protestant Sisters of Charity, later the Protestant Nursing Sisters. Five years later the Protestant Sisters of Nursing was created to work among the poor. The first purely religious nursing order of the English Church came into being in 1848 at St. John's House, London. St. John's House nurses were later to go to the Crimea with Florence Nightingale.

In 1836 in Germany, the order of deaconesses was revived. Theodor Fliedner, pastor of Kaiserswerth on the river Rhine between Duisburg and Düsseldorf, and his wife Frederika Münster fitted up a building as a hospital and a deaconess home. Its first nurse deaconess was Gertrude Reichardt (b. 1788), daughter of a doctor, whom she had assisted both in private practice and in war. Six other women became deaconesses that year.

Frau Fliedner served as superintendent of the Kaiserswerth establishment until her death. Her journal of notes on nurses' training has remained standard throughout the deaconess order. When Fliedner died in 1864 there were thirty-two deaconess houses and sixteen hundred deaconesses at work in the field.

With the advances of medicine in the eighteenth century, new nursing techniques were necessary. "The general dissatisfaction with the nursing of that day, the abortive attempts of many good people to give training to nurses, and the success of the Deaconess Order all paved the way for the coming of a woman whose ability should be equal to the task before her": Florence Nightingale.[15]

14. Florence Nightingale

Many of the nineteenth-century women who set their mark on medicine and the related sciences and occupations were inspired to a greater or lesser degree by the battle for the right of women to equal opportunity in the fields of education and medicine. Not so Florence Nightingale (1820–1910). This younger daughter of the William Nightingales of London and Embley Park wrote on one occasion: "I am brutally indifferent to the rights and wrongs of my own sex."[1]

The force that drove her to break the barriers of convention and become founder of the nursing profession as we know it today was a burning anger at needless suffering. She had nursed sick animals as a little girl. She had expressed a wish to be useful to sick persons at the age of nine. She began visiting and helping the sick poor of the neighborhood in her teens.

The activities of the typical unmarried daughter living at home in the first half of the nineteenth century were restricted to sewing, sketching, playing the piano, and going for drives in the family carriages. Fortunately for Florence and her sister, Parthenope, their father, like Samuel Blackwell, Newson Garrett, and George Palmer Putnam, believed that women possessed minds and that they should be developed. Mr. Nightingale personally tutored his daughters in Greek, Latin, philosophy, history, and mathematics. They also studied and spoke Italian, French, and German.

There was nothing unusual in Florence's visits to tenants on the Nightingale estate. It was customary for genteel ladies to drive by

in their carriages to leave food for the sick. But Florence actually
cared for the sick, feeding them, making their beds, and even rubbing
their backs. This exceeded the bounds of propriety. It wasn't even
considered safe to come in contact with such unhygienic persons.

THE DIE IS CAST

In the spring of 1844 the American humanitarian Dr. Samuel
Gridley Howe (his wife Julia would subsequently write "The Battle
Hymn of the Republic") visited the Nightingales. A conversation
Florence had with him led to a far-reaching decision.

She asked him: "Dr. Howe, do you think it would be unsuitable
and unbecoming for a young English woman to devote herself to
works of charity in hospitals and elsewhere as Catholic sisters do?
Do you think it would be a dreadful thing?"

"My dear Miss Florence," he replied, "it would be unusual, and
in England whatever is unusual is thought to be unsuitable; but I say
to you 'go forward,' if you have a vocation for that way of life, act
up to your inspiration and you will find that there is never anything
unbecoming or unladylike in doing your duty for the good of others.
Choose, go on with it, wherever it may lead you and God be with
you."[2]

Florence knew she could not mention the dread word "hospital"
to her family. She had to find an indirect means of approaching the
subject, and a year passed before she was offered an opportunity. It
was a year in which she showed herself to be completely capable—
she nursed her grandmother, and then cared for her former nurse
during her terminal illness. In the fall of 1845 there was an unusual
amount of illness in the village, and Florence devoted herself to the
care of the villagers. In December she wrote to her cousin and most
intimate friend, Hilary Bonham Carter: "I saw a poor woman die
before my eyes this summer because there was nothing but fools to
sit up with her, who poisoned her as much as if they had given her
arsenic."[3]

Florence was now ready. She broached the subject of studying nursing at Salisbury Infirmary.

The family's reaction was one of horror. Most hospitals in England catered only to the poor who had nowhere else to go. They were generally filthy, and no one who could get a job elsewhere would consider this humiliating occupation.

Florence was talked out of going to Salisbury, but she was determined to learn all she could about the condition of hospitals both in England and in continental Europe. Helped by family connections in governmental and diplomatic circles, she assembled an amazing collection of data from which to compile statistics. This was the basis for her ideas of how hospitals should be constructed and operated.

Among the material that came her way was a yearbook of the Institute of Deaconesses of Kaiserswerth. This model hospital and orphanage had seemingly eliminated the objectionable features of hospital life so greatly deplored by her family. An opportunity to visit Kaiserswerth came in 1849, when her close friends, Selina Bracebridge and her husband, proposed that she accompany them on a trip to Egypt and Greece. The Nightingales were quick to approve. Florence had recently drifted into a state of inertia. A trip might revive her, and certainly Egypt and Greece were harmless. What they did not know was that the Bracebridges planned to spend a fortnight at Düsseldorf on the way back.

When the plan was unfolded, Florence seemed too exhausted and too miserable to be enthusiastic. "On the brink of my accomplishing my greatest wish," she wrote later, "I seemed to be unfit, unmanned for it, it seemed to be not the calling for me. . . ." But after spending two weeks at Kaiserswerth she felt "so brave as if nothing could ever vex me again."[4]

Still Florence moved cautiously. It was not until 1851 that she announced to the family that she had made arrangements to study at Kaiserswerth for three months. She had made up her mind to go, with or without consent, but this time the Nightingales offered no resistance, only requesting that her stay be kept secret.

Looking back in 1897, Miss Nightingale denied that she had "trained" at Kaiserswerth. While she praised the pure devotion of the deaconesses, she wrote that the "nursing there was nil, the hygiene horrible. The hospital was certainly the worst part."[5] How fair this statement was is open to question. By 1895 she was already complaining of loss of memory, the forerunner of the mental deterioration and blindness that would cloud her final years.

FROM KAISERSWERTH TO THE CRIMEA

Her later condemnation of the caliber of nursing notwithstanding, Florence Nightingale left Kaiserswerth in October 1851 determined to train in earnest—perhaps at one of the great London hospitals. Her immediate plans were thwarted by her father, who was suffering from inflammation of the eyes. His doctor had ordered him to Worcestershire for cold-water treatments. He refused to go unless Florence accompanied him.

In 1852 she was in Dublin, where she hoped to work with the Sisters of Mercy, but she was recalled when her sister Parthe had a nervous breakdown. It has been said that Parthe "decided that if Florence must nurse somebody it might as well be herself and she threw a series of hysterical illnesses to oblige her in this respect."[6]

Florence did not stay at Embley longer than was necessary to see Parthe well cared for, but in October, when she was ready to leave for Paris to work with the Sisters of Charity, Great Aunt Evans took ill. Florence nursed her through her last illness. She finally reached Paris on February 4, 1853 where arrangements were made for her to enter the Sisters of Charity's Hospital, the Maison de la Providence, as a prelude to undertaking training in nursing. Once again she was called home, this time to nurse her dying grandmother.

In August 1853 Florence went to work as superintendent of the Institution for the Care of Sick Gentlewomen in Distressed Circumstances. This rest home was completely respectable but criminally mismanaged. To save face for the family, Florence took the post without salary. Her father responded by giving her a yearly allowance. The wealthy female board members who confirmed Miss Nightingale's appointment were delighted with the idea of a lovely, interested, dedicated young gentlewoman taking care of sick governesses and companions.

They were in for a rude shock. As a first step Florence demanded that the institution be made nonsectarian. The committee wanted it to remain strictly Church of England. The new superintendent threatened to resign and won.

It had long been the practice for buckets of hot water to be carried by hand to the various floors, for meal trays to be delivered by hand and one at a time even three flights up, while patients had no means of attracting a nurse's attention except when she was making rounds. Florence had hot water piped to each floor. A dumbwaiter elevated food trays. A button installed at each bedside activated a signal at the floor nurse's desk. Here were the beginnings of reform.

By January 1854 the institution was running smoothly, and Florence was restless. She began visiting hospitals, collecting facts on which to base a case for reforming conditions for hospital nurses. An interested party was Sidney Herbert, the Secretary of War, whose wife Liz had sponsored Florence for the post of superintendent. Herbert knew that authenticated information on bad pay and worse lodgings would alert public opinion to existing evils, but this was hard to come by. Most hospital appointments came through bribery or nepotism. To give information in support of reform would put one's job in jeopardy.

All this work was soon to be put aside. In March 1854 England, France, and Turkey declared war on Russia. Allied armies landed in the Crimea in September. Florence Nightingale's talents were needed elsewhere.

WARTIME NURSING

When the time came for the British army to embark to Varna on
the Black Sea for an attack on the great Russian naval base at
Sebastopol, there were not enough transports to carry the thirty
thousand men and their equipment. Pack animals, tents, cooking
equipment, hospital marquees, medicine chests, bedding, and stores
were left behind. Men wounded at the front paid the price of this
abandonment. Amputations were performed without anesthesia.
Surgeons worked by moonlight because there were no candles.
There was no morphine to deaden pain. Men who survived this
butchery were returned by sea to Scutari, a Turkish city across the
Bosporus from Constantinople, where the allies had established their
bases. The "hospital ships" were filled to five or six times their
capacity, and the voyage lasted one to three weeks, depending on the
weather.

At Scutari conditions were scarcely better than those behind the
battle lines. The British had thought that a small hospital, attached
to an enormous barracks turned over to them by the Turkish artil-
lery, would suffice to house the wounded. They reckoned without a
cholera epidemic, which was raging at the front. Two thousand
cholera cases more than filled the hospital. The British attempted to
convert the larger barracks into a hospital. This was an impossible
task both because it was filthy and there was no one to clean it and
because there was no hospital equipment to put in it. They used it
anyway. Men lay on the floor in the same blankets, saturated with
blood and excrement, in which they had been wrapped on the bat-
tlefield. There was no kitchen in which to prepare food for them.
There were not enough doctors to take care of them.

Actually the conditions differed little from what had only too
often prevailed in military hospitals through Britain's long history
of warfare, but former horrors had been kept secret. This time there
was a war correspondent with the army. Public opinion was aroused
by dispatches sent home by William Howard Russell and published

in *The Times.* Anger mounted when it was learned that the French wounded were being cared for by a large contingent of excellent nurses—the Sisters of Charity. The British public wished to know why able-bodied English women were not doing as much.

On October 15 Secretary of War Herbert wrote to Florence Nightingale asking if she would organize a party of nurses to leave for Scutari as soon as possible. "There is but one person in England that I know of who would be capable of organizing and superintending such a scheme," he said, adding that, if "this succeeds, an enormous amount of good will be done now, and to persons deserving everything at our hands; and a prejudice will have been broken through, and a precedent established, which will multiply the good to all time."[7] In point of fact Florence had anticipated the request. She had already organized a small private expedition of nurses prepared to sail with her for Constantinople. A letter to Liz Herbert informing the Herberts of her plan crossed Sidney's letter to her.

Had Florence Nightingale needed any incentive to accept the assignment, it was contained in Herbert's prediction that effective performance would break through prejudice against women's participation in the nursing of the sick. It never occurred to her that what Sidney Herbert had asked of her was sensational: never before had a woman been enlisted by the government to undertake an official military mission.

On October 18 the cabinet unanimously confirmed her as "Superintendent of the Female Nursing Establishment of the English General Hospitals in Turkey." Her authority was broad. The formal confirmation read: "Everything relating to the distribution of the nurses, the hours of their attendance, their allotment to particular duties is placed in your hands, subject of course to the sanction and approval of the chief medical officer; but the selection of the nurses in the first instance is placed solely under your control."[8]

On October 21, six days after receipt of Herbert's invitation, Florence Nightingale left England for Scutari accompanied by thirty-eight nurses. There were ten Roman Catholic nuns, fourteen

Anglican sisters and nurses from St. John's House, and fourteen hospital nurses. This last contingent was a sorry lot, typical of the British nursing profession in 1854. Their performance caused Miss Nightingale to write later from Scutari in respect of future recruits, "Fat drunken old dames of fourteen stone and over must be barred."[9]

On November 4 anchor was dropped in Constantinople after a frightful sea voyage in "a horrible ship . . . infested with huge cockroaches and so notorious for her discomfort that the Government had difficulty in manning her."[10]

Nothing she had heard in London had prepared her for the reality of the Scutari "hospital." It was built directly over a large cesspool that had not been drained in years. Its floors oozed with a filthy slime. The wounded lay uncared for on stinking straw mattresses crawling with vermin. There was no ventilation. "It is impossible to describe the state of the atmosphere of the Barracks Hospital at night," she wrote. "I have been well acquainted with the dwellings of the worst part of the great cities of Europe, but have never been in an atmosphere which I could compare with it." To her companions she said: "The strongest will be wanted at the washtub!"[11]

The local military officials openly resented Miss Nightingale, presuming that she had been sent out by a civilian cabinet in London to spy on them. But there was no time for petty quarrels. Transports of men wounded in the disastrous battle of Balaclava were quickly followed by the men wounded at the bloody battle of Inkerman. The medical staff panicked. The doctors were grateful for help from any source. One of them would write later: "I cannot conceive . . . how it could have been possible to avoid a state of things too disastrous to contemplate, had not Miss Nightingale been there."[12]

She was hampered by more than official hostility and human stupidity. A hurricane sank supply ships. Cholera mowed down the soldiers that the bullets spared; as many soldiers died of disease as of wounds. The death rate of cases treated was an appalling 42 percent.

Though she had little time personally to devote to nursing, it was as a nurse that the wounded knew her and loved her. "What a comfort it was to see her pass even," one soldier wrote home. "She would speak to one, and nod and smile to as many more; but she could not do it all you know. We lay there by hundreds; but we could kiss her shadow as it fell and lay our heads on the pillow again content."[13] Longfellow immortalized her as the "Lady with a Lamp," and she has been depicted walking by night through the wards with their four miles of beds. In this some poetic and artistic license is involved. "I work in the wards all day and write all night," she reported to Sidney Herbert.[14]

What she wrote involved more than demands that immediate steps be taken to improve conditions at Scutari. Determined that tragic conditions such as she had found and been forced to live with at Scutari be avoided in the future, she detailed plans for reorganizing military hospitals. She urged that a method she had worked out for keeping medical statistics at army hospitals be adopted. She proposed the establishment of an army medical school that would teach camp hygiene and military medicine.

Thanks to this unrelenting stream of reports to Herbert, a Sanitary Commission with full authority to clean up the hospital left England early in 1855. As a result of her efforts, backed by the commission, the death rate per thousand among Scutari patients fell from 430 to 22.

Florence Nightingale's stay at Scutari falls into two distinct periods. During the frightful winter of 1854–55, when her presence alone saved the hospital from collapse, opposition disappeared and she reigned supreme. But from the spring of 1855, with conditions improved and pressures lessened, petty jealousies, treacheries, and misrepresentations returned to plague her. She became obsessed by a sense of failure and was physically exhausted.

THE BATTLE FOR ARMY REFORM

Florence Nightingale returned to England in August 1856. She was primed to fight the official indifference and stupidity that had led to the tragedy she had witnessed. But the war was over and the public wanted to forget about it. Sidney Herbert joined her family and friends in telling her she must rest.

She would have none of it. "These people have fed their children on the fat of the land and dressed them in velvet and silk. . . . I have had to see my children dressed in a dirty blanket and an old pair of regimental trowsers, and to see them fed on raw salt meat; and nine thousand of my children are dying, from causes which might have been prevented, in their foreign graves! But I can never forget!"[15]

An opportunity to advance her cause came six weeks after Florence's return to England. She was summoned to Balmoral Castle in Scotland to be personally thanked for her services to the nation by Queen Victoria and the Prince Consort. Taking full advantage of the occasion, she begged the queen to persuade the cabinet to establish a royal commission to examine the health of the British army in peace and war.

The War Office now regarded Miss Nightingale as a dangerous nuisance. She had been useful in an emergency three thousand miles distant, but here at home her radical ideas could not be tolerated. Nothing was done.

Florence resorted to polite blackmail. She told Lord Panmure, who had replaced Herbert as Secretary of War, that, unless a royal commission was convened immediately and gave tangible evidence that reform would come out of their deliberations, she would in three months publish her war experiences and her suggestions for improvement.

On May 5, 1857, a royal commission was officially established. It was headed by Miss Nightingale's sponsor, Sidney Herbert. The other members were of her choosing. She not only aided them in their deliberations but made available to them facts and figures from her unpublished "Notes Affecting the Health, Efficiency, and Hospital Administration of the British Army." This monumental work covered in its twenty-one chapters such topics as deficiencies in transporting the sick, sanitary recommendations for hospitals, the employment of female nurses, the employment of male nurses, the need for special sanitary functionaries (at home and abroad), the inaccuracy of hospital statistics, the need for a statistical department, forms for medical statistics, reports on the greater mortality and morbidity rates in certain corps, notes on the education, employment, and promotion of medical officers, notes on pay and stoppages, soldiers' wives, diet and cooking, and hospital construction.

The commission's report was delivered to Lord Panmure a year to the day after her return to England. The facts it disclosed were shocking. Army conditions were almost as bad in peacetime as they were in wartime. Due to the unhealthy barracks in which the men lived, for example, the death rate among soldiers ran two to five times as great as that for neighboring civilians, even though the army enlisted the youngest and strongest of the male population.

The very thought of what public reaction might be if Miss Nightingale carried through her threat to publish her "Notes" should have brought action, but again Lord Panmure procrastinated. Nine months went by before the War Office appointed Dr. Thomas Alexander, with whom Miss Nightingale had worked at Scutari, Director General of the Medical Department of the Army and before the House of Commons passed a series of resolutions that revolutionized barrack conditions. A year later the government fell, and Sidney Herbert again became Secretary of War.

Everything Florence Nightingale had fought for seemed secure. It was agreed that sanitary arrangements in barracks and military hospitals would be remodeled to meet her specifications, that drinking water would be drinkable, and that the soldiers' diet would be made strengthening and more palatable. The army medical school would finally be established.

It was one thing to obtain the promise of reform and quite another to see it carried out. "The War Office is a very slow office, an enormously expensive office, and one in which the Minister's intentions can be entirely negatived by all his sub-departments and those of each of the sub-departments by every other," Miss Nightingale wrote in November 1859.[16]

Herbert agreed that his War Office must be reformed. Together they determined "to simplify the procedure, to abolish divided responsibility, to define clearly the duties of each head of a department and of each class of office; to hold heads responsible for their respective departments with direct communication with the Secretary of [War]." The program suffered a setback when Sidney Herbert (now Lord Herbert of Lea) died in August 1861. Almost his last coherent words, as recorded by his wife, were: "Poor Florence . . . poor Florence, our joint work unfinished."[17]

CIVILIAN NURSING

In August 1857 Florence Nightingale had suffered a complete nervous collapse that was to leave her a semi-invalid through the remaining fifty-three years of her life. This by no means spelled an end to her activities. While she was battling and then attempting totally to reorganize the War Office, she produced two books.

Notes on Hospitals (1859) was based on facts and figures collected over a period of fifteen years. She was able to show that hospital deaths were caused more frequently by hospital conditions than by entering disease. The book also revealed that she was an expert on hospital construction and management. In the next fifty years few hospitals were built anywhere in the world without her advice.

Notes on Hospitals was intended for the experts. *Notes on Nursing* (1860) was written for the housewives of England. Many aspects of household hygiene taken for granted today were first introduced in this book.

Back in 1855, when Florence Nightingale had been at the height of her popularity, a Nightingale Fund had been established. The proceeds were intended for the foundation of a training school for nurses. When Herbert had informed her of the fund's existence and asked her how she would like the organizing committee to proceed, she had replied from Scutari that she was somewhat busy at the moment but would give consideration to the project when she had time. But she never forgot that the fund existed. And now she had time.

She worked out every detail personally, but she recognized that she could not take an active part in the program because of her limited physical abilities. Direction of the school was entrusted to Mrs. Wardroper, formerly matron of St. Thomas's.

On June 24, 1860, the first group of students entered the Nightingale Training School for Nurses at St. Thomas's Hospital for a year's training. They were fifteen in number and each had a certificate of good character. Mrs. Wardroper served for twenty-seven years, and a great part of the success of the school must be attributed to her determination and energy.

On the whole the medical profession (always reactionary) was opposed to the idea. The opposition was led by Mr. J. F. South, senior consulting surgeon at St. Thomas's and president of the College of Surgeons. In his opinion, and that of many of his colleagues, a nurse, preferably a middle-aged woman, should be no more than a superior servant whose sole function was to carry out doctors' orders. She did not need to be educated. But all things change with time, and Nightingale graduates were soon going forth to head new schools of nursing all over the world.

THE "CALLING" OF NURSING

During the last fifty years of her life, Florence Nightingale was diligent in her attempt to gain public recognition of nursing as it could and should be. In 1860 she wrote: "I use the word Nursing for want of a better. It has been limited to signify little more than the administration of medicines and the applications of poultices. It ought to signify the proper use of fresh air, light, warmth, cleanliness, quiet and proper selection and administration of diet—all at least expense of vital power to the patient. . . . The art of nursing, as now practiced, seems to be expressly constituted to unmake what God has made disease to be, viz., a reparative process." And thirty years later: "Nursing is putting us in the best possible condition for nature to restore and preserve health. Health is not only to be well, but to be able to use well every power we have to use."[18]

In a paper delivered to the Nursing Section of the Congress of Hospitals, Dispensaries, and Nursing, held at the World's Fair, Chicago, in 1893, she said: "Nursing should not be a profession. It should be a *calling.*" And again: "The art is that of nursing the sick. Please mark, not nursing sickness. . . . This is the reason why nursing proper can only be taught by the patient's bedside and in the sick room or ward. Lectures and books are but valuable accessories."[19]

Since 1860 nursing schools have proliferated throughout the world. The first American nursing school was organized in 1872 at the New England Hospital for Women and Children by Dr. Marie Zakrzewska and Dr. Susan Dimock (1847–1875).

Florence Nightingale was an outstanding nurse but actively a professional nurse for only three of her ninety years. She should more properly be remembered for having founded the "calling" of nursing as it exists today.

15. Dorothea Lynde Dix

Dorothea Lynde Dix (1802–1887), who was to become known as the champion of the insane, was born on a farm on the outskirts of Hampden, six miles from Bangor in what is now Maine. Her father, Joseph Dix, had been compelled to leave Harvard and was banished to this wild, unbroken, largely uninhabited Massachusetts frontier when he married Mary Bigelow against the wishes of his father, Dr. Elijah Dix. Dr. Dix's ultimatum accomplished more than the removal of the young couple from Boston, where members of the family had already exhibited strong disapproval of Mary. It also provided an overseer for the many acres of heavily wooded land along the Penobscot River that the doctor had acquired some years earlier.

Settlers in the Hampden area were poor. Their crude log cabins usually consisted of a single room and an attic, with perhaps a lean-to. The panes of the small windows were more often of oiled paper than of glass; shutters kept out the cold of winter. A fireplace provided heat, ventilation, and light and served for cooking. Men, women, and children had to work hard to secure even the necessities of life. It was not work alone that deprived the children of the pleasures of youth. Their parents held Calvinistic beliefs that proscribed hilarity. It was not unusual for these frontier children to mature before their time. This was the world into which Dorothea Lynde Dix was born on April 4, 1802.

Joseph Dix was neither physically nor mentally fitted for frontier life. Deciding that farming and the management of his father's land were simply not for him, he began looking for another means of livelihood. He had studied theology at Harvard and he now experienced a call to preach. He packed his saddlebags and set forth "to carry the gospel to the farthest settlements."[1]

Joseph Dix was better educated than the typical Methodist minister of his day, had a pleasing personality, and spoke with deep conviction. Though his preaching brought him recognition and respect, the financial return was negligible. Unable to maintain the farm alone, Mary Dix became discouraged and unhappy. Joseph began drifting from one occupation to another, moving his family from village to village.

From time to time Dr. Elijah Dix came to look over his lands. Dorothea, neglected by an often absent father and a tired, frequently sick mother, found in Grandfather Dix all that she should have had from her parents. The relationship was cemented by the occasional visits Dorothea paid to Boston.

Dorothea was four when her brother Joseph was born. Charles Wesley followed about two years later. Their arrivals meant less attention and added chores for her. To her household responsibilities were added the folding and stitching of tracts that her father printed and sold as an additional source of income.

Dr. Dix died when Dorothea was seven. Three years later she persuaded her grandmother to let her come and live with her in Boston. The move was largely out of the frying pan into the fire. Mrs. Dix had always disliked her daughter-in-law Mary, and she could not offer Mary's child the love she so desperately needed. After two years she gave up the unequal struggle of trying to cope with a precocious child and sent Dorothea to Sarah Lynde Duncan and her daughter, Sarah Duncan Fiske, in Worcester.

This was a fortunate event for Dorothea. Aunt Sarah was a woman of tact and sympathy. Sarah Fiske was warm and understanding. Dorothea responded to their care, and her attitudes toward the tasks she was asked to perform changed.

Somehow Dorothea had acquired an education in a day when educational opportunities for girls were limited. In 1816, at the age of fourteen, she obtained her aunt's permission to start a school for little children. The pupils, who at one time numbered as many as twenty, included children of the best families in Worcester. After three years she closed the school and returned to her grandmother's house, Orange Court, in Boston, "very much improved in manners and habits of neatness."[2]

The next two years were devoted to study in preparation for a teacher's career. In 1821 she opened a school at Orange Court. Grandmother Dix initially opposed the idea. "There was no necessity, she said, for a grandaughter of Elijah Dix to wear her life away teaching school. There were other women in Boston who really needed to teach; and again there was Dorothea's health to consider." (Dorothea had early revealed a susceptibility to throat and pulmonary disorders.) She "finally gave in to her granddaughter because she loved her and had not the strength or the gift of argument to oppose her."[3]

The Orange Court school survived until the spring of 1836, when Dorothea suffered a complete nervous and physical collapse. She left for England on April 22. In the fall of 1837 she returned to claim a bequest from her grandmother who had died the previous spring.

"LUNATICS DO NOT FEEL THE COLD"

In March 1841 Dorothea Dix, aged thirty-nine, heard that someone was needed to teach a Sunday School class in the East Cambridge jail. She volunteered. After her first class she walked through the jail and talked to the female prisoners. Among them were a number of insane women whose affliction was their only crime against society. She found that there was no stove or other source of heat in their part of the jail. When she asked the jailer about it he replied that a fire would be unsafe. Besides, he said, lunatics do not feel the cold as others do.

The decision to do something about the inhumane conditions turned out to be the beginning of her life's work. Her first step was to enlist the help of a number of well-known philanthropists. After they had made their own investigation of the East Cambridge jail, one of them, Charles Sumner, wrote this account of what he saw:

> They were cramped together in rooms *poorly ventilated and noisome with filth.* . . . You cannot forget the small room in which were confined the raving maniac, from whom long since reason had fled, never to return, and the interesting young woman, whose mind was so slightly obscured that it seemed as if, in a moment, even while we were looking on, the cloud would pass away. In two cages or pens constructed of plank within the four stone walls of the same room, these two persons had spent several months. The whole prison echoes with the blasphemies of the poor old woman, while her young and gentle fellow in suffering, doomed to spend her days and nights in such close connection with her, seemed to shrink from her words as from blows. And well she might; for they were words not to be heard by any woman in whom reason had left any vestige of its former presence. It was a punishment by a cruel man in heathen days to tie the living to the dead; hardly less horrid was this scene in the prison at Cambridge.[4]

Actually these conditions were not unusual. There were then few hospitals maintained at public expense that even pretended to give the mentally ill scientific treatment in relatively pleasant surroundings. Poor farms and jails, where they were housed with criminals, vagrants, and paupers, were the fate of indigent psychotics. The 1840 census classified as insane 17,434 out of a population of 23,292,876, and these must largely have been indigent persons, since the well-to-do took care of and concealed their own. The "asylums" for the mentally ill maintained by a few states and some cities were rarely more than specialized almshouses.

Though an occasional hospital was doing good work, a great

majority of the mentally ill were without medical treatment that could in any sense be rated scientific or humane. The Worcester (Massachusetts) Hospital, opened in 1835, was one of these few. Under the supervision of Dr. Samuel Woodward, in eight years it cared for over a thousand patients, of whom close to half were restored to health and usefulness. But the Worcester Hospital could not begin to take care of all the mental defectives in Massachusetts.

Through the efforts of Samuel Eliot, who became mayor of Boston in 1837, the Boston Lunatic Asylum began operating on December 11, 1839. Yet fifteen months later Dorothea could uncover the shocking conditions in the East Cambridge jail, less than an hour's walk from the Boston asylum.

Miss Dix Acts in Massachusetts

Dorothea took the East Cambridge case to court. As an outcome heat was provided and the quarters of the insane were renovated. She was encouraged to find the inmates calmer and less afraid. The more she visited these "prisoners" the more she wondered about conditions in other prisons and almshouses. Trips to nearby towns convinced her that a survey of the state would reveal far worse abuses. She decided to undertake a survey at her own expense, and within a dozen miles of Boston she saw unfortunate human beings "confined in cages, closets, cellars, stalls, pens . . . chained, naked, beaten with rods, and lashed into obedience. . . ." She encountered a young woman who, before her mind was shaken, had been respectable, industrious, and worthy. "There she stood, clinging to, or beating upon, the bars of her caged apartment, the contracted size of which afforded space only for increasing accumulation of filth— a *foul* spectacle; there she stood, with naked arms and dishevelled hair; the unwashed frame invested with fragments of unclean garments; the air so extremely offensive, though ventilation was afforded on all sides save one, that it was not possible to remain beyond a few moments without retreating for recovery to the outward air. Irritation of body, produced by utter filth and exposure, incited her to the horrid process of tearing off her skin by inches; her face, neck, and person were thus disfigured to hideousness. She held up a fragment just rent off. To my exclamation of horror, the mistress replied, 'Oh, we can't help it. . . . We can do nothing with her; and it makes no difference what she eats, for she consumes her own filth as readily as the food which is brought her.' "[5]

Moving farther afield, Miss Dix found at the Westford poorhouse a young woman sitting on the floor, her naked body partly covered by an old blanket. "Around her waist was a heavy chain, the end of which was attached to the wall. As Miss Dix entered, the young woman blushed and tried to draw about her the insufficient fragments of the blanket. Miss Dix knelt beside the girl and asked if she did not want to be dressed. 'Yes, I want some clothes.' 'But you will tear 'em all up, you know you will,' interposed the caretaker. 'No, I won't, I won't tear them off,' screamed the girl as she started to rise. The chain pulled her down again, and pointing to it, she burst forth in a wild shrill laugh, 'See there, nice clothes.' Despite her appeals for clothes, the attendant only sneered and ignored the piteous request."[6]

By the end of 1842 Miss Dix had visited, at least once, every almshouse, workhouse, and prison in the state of Massachusetts. She found the same appalling conditions everywhere. She was ready to write her memorial to the legislature. "I come to present the strong claim of suffering humanity," it began.[7]

The memorial was presented in January 1843. The opposition that developed was out of all proportion. Miss Dix was learning firsthand that society is affronted by any unpleasant truth that casts reflection on its self-righteousness, especially when the resolution of the truth will increase taxes. Everywhere the overseers of the poor vehemently accused her of slanderous sensationalism. The situations described were said to be "impossible in a community such as ours."[8]

The legislature postponed debate from day to day until February 25. Then, finding the cause backed by such respected citizens as

Charles Sumner, the orator and statesman, the educator Horace Mann, and Dr. Luther V. Bell of McLean Psychiatric Hospital, the committee to which the memorial was referred endorsed it for immediate action.

When the content of the committee's report became known, the public came to its senses and acknowledged the deplorable local conditions. Politicians withdrew their objections, and the bill for immediate relief of the mentally ill was passed by a good majority.

THE CRUSADE IS BROADENED

In the course of her investigations in Massachusetts, Miss Dix often crossed the borders into the neighboring states of New York, Rhode Island, and Connecticut. In January 1844 she presented a memorial to the New York state legislature. She would have presented one to the Rhode Island legislature as well if private philanthropy had not offered speedier relief.

When Nicholas Brown, the founder of Brown University, died in 1843 he left thirty thousand dollars to be used for building and maintaining a retreat for the insane in Providence. This was not enough, and Miss Dix set out to raise more.

She approached Cyrus Butler, an old bachelor worth millions with a reputation for being stingy. "I want you to give fifty thousand dollars toward the enlargement of the insane hospital in this city, to be called henceforth Butler Asylum," she told him.[9] Butler replied that he would give forty thousand if a like sum were pledged by responsible individuals within six months. Thanks to her efforts, the conditional sum was oversubscribed.

What spurred Rhode Islanders to action was the case of Abraham Simmons of Little Compton. Miss Dix found him in a seven-foot-square cell, the stone walls and floor of which were coated with frost. Even the floor was of stone, and there were double walls and double doors because, the attendant explained, his "cries disturb us in the house." Simmons was "tethered to the floor by an ox chain."[10]

In an article in the *Providence Journal* for April 10, 1844, Miss Dix, after describing the "suffering and tortures . . . of Abraham Simmons," issued this challenge: "Should any persons in this philanthropic age be disposed from motives of curiosity to visit the place they may rest assured that traveling is considered quite safe in that part of the country, however improbable it may seem."

Though she was often ill she worked tirelessly. On March 25, 1845, the New Jersey legislature authorized the construction of a state lunatic asylum. In a "Memorial Soliciting a State Hospital for the Insane of Pennsylvania," submitted at Harrisburg on February 3, 1845, Miss Dix declared that the Allegheny county jail in Pittsburgh combined the faults and abuses of the worst county prisons in the United States. On April 15 the legislature voted to establish the Pennsylvania State Lunatic Hospital at Harrisburg.

In three years, she traveled more than ten thousand miles by stage, steamboat, railroad, and even on horseback. Only a courageous, determined woman could have withstood these rigors. Once she was almost drowned in a stage fording a river. There was, on occasion, a brighter side. When robbers held up her stage in Michigan, she told them how foolish they were. One of them recognized the voice of the woman who had spoken in the insane ward of a Philadelphia jail when he was imprisoned there. The loot was promptly returned.

Miss Dix wanted to know all there was to know about the causes of mental disease and how it could be treated. She spent as much time as she could reading books on the subject. Innkeepers would bank the fire and retire for the night, leaving her to read by the light of a candle or a sperm-oil lamp. Hours of waiting at lonely junctions between stages and trains became hours of study.

As she made her way through the country she harassed and charmed, praised and condemned. She pleaded with the legislatures of New Jersey, Pennsylvania, Illinois, Kentucky, Tennessee, Mississippi, Louisiana, Alabama, the Carolinas, and Maryland. Asylums sprang up in her wake. Sadistic thugs were replaced by doctors who believed that something could be done for mental cases.

A PRESIDENTIAL VETO

In the mid-1840s Miss Dix worked out a plan to provide for the mentally ill, both immediately and in the future, based on the use of public land. It was the established policy of the federal government to grant tracts of land to new states for the institution of improvements, including the establishment of schools. By 1845 about one hundred and thirty-five million acres of public domain had been ceded to the states, but over one hundred million acres remained. Why not put a part of this in trust for the indigent insane, Miss Dix asked. A government that provided schools, homesteads, and highways for the sane surely owed something to the destitute insane.

A memorial was presented to Congress on June 27, 1848. She initially asked that some twelve million acres be set aside, but the longer Congress procrastinated the more she asked. By 1852 the request for acreage had been doubled, and she was also asking for a hundred thousand dollars for a hospital to take care of the insane of the army, the navy, and the District of Columbia.

On March 9, 1854, a bill embodying her requests passed the Senate by a good majority. It looked as if fourteen years' effort was about to come to fruition. When word came that the House of Representatives had also passed the bill, she was jubilant. All that was now needed was the signature of President Franklin Pierce, and he had personally expressed interest in the project. His decision to veto the bill was a bitter surprise to its many supporters.

President Pierce declared in his veto message that he had been "compelled to resist the deep sympathies of his own heart in favor of the humane purposes sought to be accomplished. . . ." There were, however, larger issues. "If Congress have power to make provision for indigent insane *without the limits of this district,* it has the same power to provide for the indigent who are not insane and thus to transfer to the federal government the charge of *all the poor in all the states. . . .* The fountains of charity will be dried up at home, and the several States, instead of bestowing their own means on the social wants of their own people, may themselves become humble suppli- cants for the bounty of the federal government, reversing their true relation to this Union."[11]

In July the veto was sustained. Dorothea Lynde Dix had lost her greatest battle.

TRAVELS ABROAD

Miss Dix's impulse was to get out of Washington, but there were commitments she had to meet. By September she was free to sail for Liverpool. There she was met by old friends. William Rathbone, a former mayor of Liverpool, and his wife took her to their home, Greenbank, a beautiful country estate. Dorothea promised to rest here for a month. To turn a philanthropic crusader into a tourist was impossible. In less than a fortnight she was "much occupied with charitable institutions and the meetings of the British Scientific As- sociation. All this tires me sadly but I shall take things easier in a week. It is my purpose to go to Scotland to see the hospitals in ten days."[12]

The condition of the insane in Scotland left much to be desired. Hospitals for the mentally ill were badly in need of reform. "I came here for pleasure but that is no reason why I should close my eyes to the condition of these most helpless of all God's creatures. . . . I am confident that [reform] is to rest with me and that the sooner I address myself to this work of humanity the sooner will my con- science cease to suggest effort, or rebuke inaction."[13]

Her English friends had discouraged her decision to survey the Scottish institutions, telling her that she would be regarded as an impertinent stranger. But on April 9, 1855, her efforts were re- warded when Queen Victoria appointed a commission to investigate the status of the insane in Scotland.

Her next attack was on conditions prevailing on Jersey in the

Channel Islands. The outcome was a hospital for the insane. True, it was not completed until 1869, but without Miss Dix's proddings it would never have been begun.

Dorothea, persuaded to go to Switzerland for a couple of months of rest, decided then to tour the hospitals, prisons, and insane asylums in Europe. She planned to go as far as Turkey and perhaps the Holy Land—a long-cherished dream.

In Paris, where no restrictions were placed on her visits, she was pleasantly surprised to find only two faults in the conduct of the various institutions: they lacked ventilation and the treatment undertaken by the interns was of a highly experimental character.

In Naples, she found a hospital for the mentally ill that outshone all others in Italy. On the other hand, she was particularly shocked by what she encountered in the shadow of the Vatican. She secured an audience with Pope Pius IX, who promised personally to investigate the horrors she described. At a second audience he thanked her for having called his attention to the miseries of the mentally ill in his flock.

Miss Dix reached Constantinople in April 1856. She had heard tales of horrible suffering in Turkish prisons and hospitals, but after inspecting all the hospitals and prisons and a psychopathic hospital, run by a Turk who had trained in Paris, she wrote Mrs. Rathbone: "The insane of Constantinople are in better condition than those of Rome or Trieste, and in some respects better cared for than in Turin, Milan, or Ancona. . . . The provisions for the comfort and pleasure of the patients, including music, quite astonished me. The superintendent proposes improvements. I had substantially little to suggest and nothing to urge."[14]

Her idea of going to Jerusalem was abandoned as a personal luxury. She confined her "journeys to those places where hospitals or the want of them" called her.[15] By the time she returned to England on August 1, she had visited Paris, Naples, Rome, Florence, Trieste, Turin, Venice, Cyprus, Constantinople, Budapest,

Vienna, Moscow, St. Petersburg, Christiania, Stockholm, Brussels, and Amsterdam. Toward the end of September she sailed back to America.

To the End

In the years immediately prior to the Civil War, Miss Dix kept an ear close to the ground as she traveled back and forth across the country. She encountered religious zealots, abolitionists, free-traders, and politicians of a variety of hues. The fact that she did not take sides did not mean that she did not have strong personal convictions, but she felt that she must not jeopardize her central cause. Her responsibility was to the insane. She surveyed almshouses in Toronto, selected the site for St. Elizabeth's Hospital in Washington, D.C., inspected jails and almshouses in Texas, and attempted to get state legislatures in the South to appropriate a third of a million dollars for hospitals.

When the war broke out in April 1861, Miss Dix put aside her main concern and volunteered to recruit nurses for the Union Army. On April 23 Secretary of War Cameron accepted her offer. On June 10 she was commissioned Superintendent of United States Army Nurses. Almost sixty and never in good health, she nevertheless tackled the assignment with her usual vigor and served throughout the war. Her work received recognition on December 3, 1866. The Secretary of War, now Edwin M. Stanton, issued an order that read:

> In token and acknowledgement of the inestimable services rendered by Miss Dorothea L. Dix for the care, succor, and relief of the sick and wounded soldiers of the United States on the battlefield, in camps, and hospitals during the recent war, and of her benevolent and diligent labors and devoted efforts to whatever might contribute to their comfort and welfare, it is ordered that a stand of arms of the United States colors be presented to Miss Dix.[16]

The year 1867 found Miss Dix again inspecting jails, poorhouses, and institutions for the mentally ill. During the next fifteen years she traversed the country from Maine to Florida, from New York to California. In 1877, when she was seventy-five, Dr. Charles Folsom wrote in his *Diseases of the Mind:* "Her frequent visits to our institutions of the insane now, and her searching criticisms, constitute of themselves a better lunacy commission than would be likely to be appointed in many of our states."[17]

In October 1881, after still another exhausting journey of inspection through New York and New England, she went for a rest to the New Jersey State Hospital at Trenton, which she had been instrumental in setting up in 1848. She never left it again. She lingered on for five years. On the evening of July 18, 1887, she died.

That Miss Dix and her work have largely been forgotten, "is due in part to Miss Dix herself. She never permitted any personal interviews or what would today be called publicity. She would allow no asylum to be named for her. . . . She was likely the most distinguished . . . woman that America has produced in three hundred years and more. . . . [If she] had not been born when she was, the care of the insane in the United States might well have been delayed another half century."[18]

Over her grave in Mount Auburn cemetery, near Boston, fly the American flag and the standard of the Corps of Army Nurses. The simple marble marker reads DOROTHEA L. DIX—without dates or epitaph.

16. Jane Addams

The relationship of Jane Addams (1860–1935) to medicine may at first glance seem remote, but, in effect her creation, Hull-House, was practicing "preventive medicine" before that term came into popular use.

Jane was born in Cedarville, Illinois, one of the younger members of a large family. Her earliest recollections were of her Quaker father, John H. Addams (d. 1881), a dominant individual who greatly influenced her. Her mother had died when she was a baby, and her father did not marry again for eight years.

Jane was under seven years of age when she discovered that all the streets of "the little city of ten thousand people . . . were not as bewilderingly attractive as the one which contained the glittering toyshop and the confectioners." The occasion was a visit with her father to a mill located in the poorest quarter of the neighboring town. "On that day I had my first sight of the poverty which implies squalor, and felt the curious distinction between the ruddy poverty of the country and that which even a small city presents in its shabbiest streets. I remember launching at my father the pertinent inquiry why people lived in such horrid little houses so close together, and that after receiving his explanation I declared with much firmness when I grew up I should, of course, have a large house, but it would not be built among the other large houses, but right in the midst of the horrid little houses like these."[1]

At the Rockford seminary, attended by three older sisters before

Jane went there in 1877, she met girls who were ready to discuss everything under the sun. Their enthusiasms were not all talk. One was to marry a missionary and found an excellent school for American and English children in Japan; a second would become a medical missionary in Korea and, after successfully treating the queen, court physician; a third would prove an unusually skillful teacher of the blind; a fourth, a librarian, would pioneer in bringing books to the people. Unquestionably Jane Addams's choice of schoolgirl friends led her in the direction of the settlement work that would be her life. "Curiously enough," she tells us, "the actual activities of a missionary school are not unlike many that are carried on in a Settlement situated in a foreign quarter. Certainly the most sympathetic and comprehending visitors we ever had at Hull-House have been returned missionaries."[2]

Jane graduated from Rockford in the summer of 1881 with the intention of entering medicine. To this end, she spent the following winter at the Woman's Medical College of Pennsylvania. However, she had from earliest childhood suffered from curvature of the spine, and in the late spring of 1882 this disability appears to have become complicated by nervous disease. She entered the hospital of S. Weir Mitchell, the leading American neurologist of his time, who in 1875 had introduced the "Weir Mitchell treatment" for nervous disease. The treatment, which had promptly been accorded worldwide acceptance, included prolonged rest in bed. The following winter, Jane Addams reports, "I was literally bound to a bed in my sister's house for six months." This was a turning point for the would-be doctor, who admitted later that "after the first few weeks I was able to read with a luxurious consciousness of leisure, and I remember opening the first volume of Carlyle's Frederick the Great with a lively sense of gratitude that it was not Gray's Anatomy." A two-year convalescence in Europe followed. "Before I returned to America I had discovered that there were other genuine reasons for living among the poor than that of practicing medicine upon them, and my brief foray into the profession was never resumed."[3]

Early in her stay in England, Miss Addams joined a small party of tourists taken by a city missionary to the East End of London to witness the Saturday night sale of decaying fruit and vegetables that could not be held over in the stores until Monday. The wretchedness of East London made an ineradicable impression on her. "The following weeks," she wrote, "I went about London almost furtively, afraid to look down narrow streets and alleys lest they disclose again this hideous human need and suffering. I carried away with me for days at a time that curious surprise we experience when we first come back into streets after days given over to sorrow and death; we are bewildered that the world should be going on as usual and unable to determine which is real, the inner pang or the outward seeming. In time all huge London came to seem unreal save the poverty in its East End. During the following two years on the continent, while I was irresistibly drawn to the poorer quarters of each city, nothing among the beggars of South Italy nor among the saltminers of Austria carried with it the same conviction of human wretchedness which was conveyed by this momentary glimpse of an East London street."[4]

After her two years in Europe, Miss Addams spent two years in America. Toward the end of 1886 she returned to Europe for a further two years of travel and observation.

Miss Addams was unable later to recall when the thought first occurred to her "to rent a house in a part of the city where many primitive and actual needs are found, in which young women who had been given over too exclusively to study, might restore a balance of activity along traditional lines and learn of life from life itself; where they might try out some of the things they had been taught." It may have been before the second trip to Europe, or it may have been as late as April 1888, when her party reached Madrid and she remembers mentioning the plan—almost certainly for the first time. This revelation was inspired by her reaction to a bullfight, "where greatly to my surprise and horror, I found that I had seen, with comparative indifference, five bulls and many more horses killed."[5]

She resolved on the following day to put her plan into operation, if only by talking about it. The recipient of her confidence was Ellen Gates Starr (1860–1940), an old school friend who was a member of the present party. Miss Starr proved an enthusiastic listener. When they parted in Paris in June 1888 the possibility seemed strong that Ellen Starr would join Jane Addams in turning a hazy scheme into a vital reality.

What was this plan? At this stage Jane Addams scarcely knew. But four years later (1892) she could define the work she had undertaken to a meeting of the Ethical Culture Societies at Plymouth, Massachusetts in these words:

> The Settlement, then, is an experimental effort to aid in the solution of the social and industrial problems which are engendered by the modern conditions of life in the great city. It insists that these problems are not confined to any one portion of a city. It is an attempt to relieve, at the same time, the overaccumulation at one end of society and the destitution at the other; but it assumes that this overaccumulation and destitution is [sic] most sorely felt in the things that pertain to social and educational advantages. . . . The one thing to be dreaded in the Settlement is that it lose its flexibility, its power of quick adaption, its readiness to change its methods as its environment may demand. It must be open to conviction and must have a deep and abiding sense of tolerance. It must be hospitable and ready for experiment. It should demand from its residents a scientific patience in the accumulation of facts and the steady holding of their sympathies as one of the best instruments for that accumulation. It must be grounded in a philosophy whose foundation is on the solidarity of the human race, a philosophy which will not waver when the race happens to be represented by a drunken woman or an idiot boy. Its residents . . . must be content to live quietly side by side with their neighbors, until they grow into a sense of relationship and

mutual interests. Their neighbors are held apart by differences
of race and language which the residents can more easily
overcome. . . . In short, residents are pledged to devote themselves to the duties of good citizenship and to the arousing of
the social energies which too largely lie dormant in every
neighborhood given over to industrialism.[6]

HULL-HOUSE

January 1889 found Miss Addams and Miss Starr in Chicago,
ready to establish a settlement, a term borrowed from London (with
its Toynbee Hall and People's Palace, both of which Miss Addams
had studied) for an institution providing community services in
depressed areas. Concurrently they were seeking friends for the
venture. They made no appeal for money since they intended at least
to start with their own limited resources. The reception accorded
their speeches was courteous and friendly, if sometimes skeptical.

One critic attacked the plan as being "one of those unnatural
attempts to understand life through coöperative living." The organ-
izers retorted that collective living was not an essential ingredient.
Since each participant was to meet his own expenses, the time might
come when they might decide to live singly throughout the neighborhood. Miss Addams was quick to admit, however, that the critic
had a point. Community living had been known to turn the residents
inward toward companionship instead of outward toward the environment. Still, she felt this possibility was outweighed by the fact
"that the mere foothold of a house, easily accessible, ample in space,
hospitable and tolerant in spirit, situated in the midst of the large
foreign colonies which so easily isolate themselves in American
cities, would be in itself a serviceable thing for Chicago."[7]

The choice of location finally fell on a house near the intersection
of Blue Island Avenue and Halsted and Harrison Streets, on the
north side of what is now the University of Illinois Circle Campus.
The house had been built in 1856 as the homestead of a pioneer

Chicagoan, Charles J. Hull. In the years that followed it had passed through a number of hands. It had served as a home for the aged run by the Little Sisters of the Poor. It had been a secondhand furniture store. Now its lower part was used as offices and store-rooms for a factory that stood back of it. It was even said that the attic was haunted. True or not, the second-floor tenants kept a pitcher full of water on the attic stairs in the belief that ghosts could not cross water.

To begin with, Miss Addams and her friends sublet the second floor and what had been the first-floor drawing-room of this capacious house. The following year its owner, Miss Helen Culver, gener-ously gave them a freehold lease of the entire house. Nor was her generosity limited to this gift. Miss Addams could report in 1929 that "the group of thirteen buildings, which at present comprises our equipment, is built largely upon land which Miss Culver has put at the service of the Settlement which bears Mr. Hull's name."[8]

By September 18, 1889, Hull-House was furnished and ready and Miss Addams, Miss Starr, and a Miss Mary Keyser moved in. The last was engaged to do the housework but, in the five remaining years of her life, became a very important personage in the neighborhood and in the work of Hull-House.

What motivated young men and women to live in the "slums" and use their own money to further a cause? Miss Addams believed that there were three major motives. The first was a desire to interpret democracy in social terms; the second, an impulse to aid in the forward progress of our race; the third, humanitarianism. She con-cluded that the subjective necessity for social settlements is identical with the necessity that urges individuals toward social and personal salvation.[9]

OBJECTIVES ACHIEVED

The stated objectives of the undertaking, as subsequently set forth in its charter, were to "provide a center for a higher civic and social

life; to institute and maintain educational and philanthropic enter-
prises, and to investigate and improve the conditions in the industrial districts of Chicago."[10] These are cold words in contrast to the
warm reality.

Hull-House stood on the edge of several foreign colonies. About
ten thousand Italians were crowded between Halsted Street and the
Chicago River. To the south were Germans and Bohemians. The
side streets were given over to Polish and Russian Jews. French
Canadians lived to the northwest; the Irish and first-generation
Americans to the north. Among the poorer elements of each group
were those whose fortunes and positions had, for one reason or
another, declined. These were the first people helped by the volun-
teers who flocked to the Hull-House banner as soon as it was un-
furled. Reading parties and other intellectual pursuits were organized for these unfortunates who had enjoyed better days.

It was a beginning, but there were more practical needs to be
faced. There were infants and children unavoidably neglected by
mothers who worked in sweat shops. There were the children who
played in unsanitary streets and the children who worked in the
factories. There was tenement housing. There were the old people,
neglected and forlorn, who lived in dread of the poorhouse. Finally,
places for social intercourse other than the nearby saloon must be
provided.

Hull-House could not do it all. It could not feed all the hungry,
clothe the naked, house the desolate, and heal the sick. What Miss
Addams, Miss Starr, and other dedicated residents did was to draw
the attention of public authority to the deficiencies and inspire the
charitable to direct their good works where they were needed.

For its own part, Hull-House's first step was to open a kindergar-
den. This was supplemented by a public kitchen to feed the children
of working women, whose lunch might otherwise have come from
the candystore. Boys' clubs and sewing circles for girls were organized. They danced in the gymnasium, and the public kitchen
beneath it became a coffee shop. The gymnasium and coffee shop

were also used for adult gatherings, including a New Year's party for the old people living in the neighborhood. Hull-House sponsored a boarding club for working girls and even attempted to run a cooperative coal association. Soon it became known that the residents of Hull-House were ready to perform the humblest of neighborhood services—to wash newborn babes, to prepare the dead for burial, to nurse the sick, and to mind the children.

Children worked in factories from seven in the morning to nine at night under conditions that were grossly unsafe. But there was no compensation for injury or even death. Before a child could go to work, the parent was required to sign a waiver of claims for damages resulting from "carelessness." Mrs. Florence Kelley, an early Hull-House resident, prompted the Illinois State Bureau of Labor to investigate the sweat-shop system in Chicago, especially as it involved child labor. These investigations led to Illinois's first factory law.

In the 1890s garbage was accumulated in huge wooden boxes fastened to the pavement and collected periodically. In such neighborhoods as that in which Hull-House was located the system was not merely inadequate, but positively unhygienic. The normal amount of waste was swollen by decayed fruits and vegetables discarded by the Italian and Greek peddlers, and by rags so filthy that they were of no use to ragpickers who had filched them from the city dump with an eye to reconstitution. What made things worse was the fact that children played in and about these huge garbage boxes, and children ate everything they could lay their hands on. Hull-House worked for the removal of the boxes and the installation of a better system for garbage collection.

Another battle undertaken by the Hull-House residents involved the sale of cocaine to minors. The existing laws were inadequate. New legislation was finally secured in 1907.

A concerted effort was made to alert the public to the wretched conditions existing in tenement housing, and at least some landlords were influenced toward improvement. But conditions remained so bad that, during an epidemic of typhoid in 1902, the ward in which Hull-House was located, though it comprised only 3 percent of the population of Chicago, suffered 17 percent of the deaths. Hull-House residents investigated the plumbing in the areas of greatest fever concentration. They were led by Dr. Alice Hamilton, who made a bacteriological study of the various systems of plumbing and non-plumbing. She demonstrated, among other things, that conditions that encouraged the infection to spread so widely could only have existed if the city inspector was criminally negligent or in the pay of the landlords. The disclosure resulted in a civil service board trial of half the employees in the Sanitary Bureau, and eleven out of the force of twenty-four were discharged. "The inspector in our neighborhood was a kindly old man, greatly distressed over the affair, and quite unable to understand why he should not have used his discretion as to the time when a landlord should be forced to put in modern appliances. If he was 'very poor,' or 'just about to sell his place,' or 'sure that the house would be torn down to make room for a factory,' why should one 'inconvenience' him?"[11] This investigation reached into the heart of graft, in and out of city hall, and some large contributors to Hull-House withdrew their support.

Hull-House did not give up. Its staff continued to work toward better health for the community, and through its various social and educational programs, for young and old, toward the well-being of individuals new to the American culture.

The child Jane Addams told her father that she would "have a large house . . . right in the midst of the horrid little houses." She more than fulfilled her promise.

17. Marie Curie

Polish women have made medical history in various parts of the world. Marie E. Zakrzewska came by way of Berlin to the United States to set her mark on medicine. A hundred years earlier, Salomée Anne Roussietska (or Rusiecka), trained to serve as an assistant to her husband, a German oculist named Halpir, so far outstripped him that she became a famous specialist in cataract surgery in Constantinople in her own right. Mélanie Lipinska studied medicine at the University of Paris in the 1890s and became a medical historian. There were many more. But the brightest stone in the diadem was Lipinska's contemporary at the University of Paris, Marya Sklodovska, better known as Marie Curie (1867–1934), whose discovery of radium broadened the scope of therapy for cancer.

Marya was born in Warsaw, the youngest of five children of Vladislav Sklodovski, professor of physics and under-inspector of a public school. Both her parents were descended from families of the minor nobility which the misfortunes of Poland had ruined.

A century earlier Prussia, Austria, and Russia had dismembered the country. In 1831 and 1863 there had been futile attempts in Russian Poland, which embraced Warsaw, to throw off the foreign yoke, but spades, scythes, and clubs had inevitably lost to Czarist rifles. Still Poland refused to die. What could not be won in battle must be brought about by more subtle means. The peasant rebels gave place to the schoolteachers, the poets, and priests. They outwardly bowed to the Czar's dictates in order secretly to influence, guide, and instruct the youth of Poland. Schoolteachers were re-

quired to teach in the Russian language. In Mlle. Sikorska's private
school, which Marya attended, Polish history, in Polish, was taught
surreptitiously—with teachers alert for the signal bell warning of an
approaching Russian inspector.

During Marya's schoolgirl years the family saw little but tragedy.
Her father was fired from his secondary job of under-inspector by
his Russified superior, which stripped him of the free lodgings he
and his family had enjoyed. His salary as a teacher was now insufficient, and after several moves he settled his family in an apartment
large enough to take in boarders. He also gave private instruction
in order to support his family. In January 1876 two of Marya's older
sisters contracted typhoid. The elder of the two died. This was
Marya's first encounter with death. On May 9, 1878, Mme. Sklodovska died of tuberculosis, which she had contracted about the time
Marya was born.

The family survived these repeated blows, and by 1882 Marya was
rated one of the most brilliant students at the government *gymnasium*. This school, run in accordance with the Russifying spirit of
the times, was very different from Mlle. Sikorska's profoundly Polish
seminary for young ladies, but the switch had been unavoidable.
Only the imperial *gymnasia* could bestow recognized diplomas.
Marya graduated on June 12, 1883, the proud possessor of a coveted
gold medal.

STUDY IN PARIS

The University of Warsaw was closed to women. Marya dreamed
of going to France, where "liberty was cherished, all feelings and all
beliefs respected, and there was a welcome for the unhappy and the
hunted, no matter whence they came."[1] But it was not until late in
1891, after several dreary years of serving as governess in the provinces, that Marya felt free to join her sister Bronya, who was already
in Paris studying medicine and had married Casimir Dluski, a recently graduated doctor, ten years her senior.

On November, 3, 1891, Marie Sklodovska, as she now styled herself, began courses in the Faculty of Science at the Sorbonne. It was not long before her brother-in-law was writing to her father in Poland: "Mademoiselle Marie is working seriously; she passes nearly all her time at the Sorbonne and we meet only at the evening meal. She is a very independent young person, and in spite of the formal power of attorney by which you placed her under my protection, she not only shows me no respect or obedience, but does not care about my authority and my seriousness at all. I hope to reduce her to reason, but up to now my pedagogical talents have not proved efficacious. In spite of all this we understand each other very well and live in the most perfect agreement."[2]

Marie was too shy to seek friends among the French. She associated with Polish students, as poor as she, who had established a small free Poland in the Latin Quarter, into which Marie shortly moved in order to be near the university, the laboratories, and the libraries.

The fact that Marie in her attic room sometimes starved herself to the point of fainting was not entirely due to poverty. She simply was no housekeeper, not even knowing how to make soup, some said. But her lack of appetite for food was balanced by her rapacity for work. She carried a heavy load of courses in mathematics, physics, and chemistry. A perfectionist with a will of iron, she had decided to obtain not one master's degree but two. Almost incredibly, she placed first in the master's examination in physics in 1893 and second in the master's in mathematics in 1894.

PIERRE CURIE

At the beginning of 1894 the Society for the Encouragement of National Industry engaged Marie to make a study of the magnetic properties of various steels. The laboratory she was using soon became too crowded to hold the cumbersome equipment necessary for the analysis of group samples of metals. Joseph Kovalski, professor of physics at the University of Fribourg, whose young wife Marie had met during her governess days, was visiting Paris. Hearing of Marie's problem, Professor Kovalski invited her to come to tea after dinner the following evening to meet a promising young scientist he had encountered at the School of Physics and Chemistry who might have a room available there. Here are the words with which Marie described her first encounter with Pierre Curie (1859–1906):

> When I came in, Pierre Curie was standing in the window recess near a door leading to the balcony. He seemed very young to me, although he was then aged thirty-five. I was struck by the expression of his clear gaze and by a slight appearance of carelessness in his lofty stature. His rather slow, reflective words, his simplicity, and his smile, at once grave and young, inspired confidence. A conversation began between us and became friendly; its object was some questions of science upon which I was happy to ask his opinion.[3]

Pierre Curie was born in Paris, the son of Dr. Eugène Curie, himself the son of a doctor. By 1894 Pierre, though largely unknown in France, was respected by foreign colleagues as a scientific genius. In August 1893, for example, an illustrious English scientist, Lord Kelvin, had traveled to Paris at the age of sixty-nine to hear Curie report to the Physics Society and went out of his way to meet the young physicist. On his return home he wrote to Pierre:

> I thank you very much for having taken the trouble to obtain for me an apparatus by which I can so conveniently observe the magnificent experimental discovery of piezoelectric quartz, made by you and your brother.
>
> I have written a note for the *Philosophical Magazine*, making it clear that your work preceded mine. This note should arrive in time to appear in the October number, but if not it will certainly appear in November.[4]

Pierre had received his Bachelor of Science degree at sixteen and his master's degree at eighteen. He was appointed a laboratory assistant in the Faculty of Medicine at nineteen and worked with his brother Jacques, also a laboratory assistant. Their piezoelectric quartz apparatus, to which Lord Kelvin referred, was designed to permit the precise measurement of small quantities of electricity.

In 1883 the brothers had regretfully separated, Jacques to become a professor at Montpellier and Pierre chief of laboratory at the School of Physics and Chemistry of the City of Paris. Pierre went on to make important discoveries in crystalline physics and magnetism.

MARRIAGE

At the meeting arranged by the Kovalskis, Pierre felt intensely curious about the foreign girl who had so little to say. He had, however, asked if he might visit her, and before Marie returned to Poland for the summer he proposed marriage.

Marie declined. She was Polish by birth and a political activist by upbringing. To abandon home and family and marry a Frenchman would be an act of betrayal.

The young scientist refused to be discouraged by his rejection or her departure. All summer long he bombarded her with letters. When she returned to Paris in October he renewed his personal campaign. Ten more months passed before she accepted the idea of marriage.

Marie declared that the wedding, which would take place on July 26, 1895, was to be "different from all other weddings. There was to be no white dress, no gold ring, no 'wedding breakfast.' " There would be no religious ceremony: Pierre was a freethinker, and Marie, for a long time past, had ceased the practices of religion. There were no lawyers necessary, as the marriage pair possessed nothing in the world—nothing but two glittering bicycles, bought the day before with money sent as a present by a cousin, with which they were going to roam the countryside in the coming summer.[5]

On September 12, 1897, Marie gave birth to Irène, who, with her future husband Frédéric Joliot, would receive the Nobel Prize for chemistry in 1935. The thought of choosing between family life and a scientific career never entered Marie's mind. Love, maternity, and science must function compatibly in her life. There was no other way. Within three months of Irène's birth, Mme. Curie had completed her paper on magnetism for the *Bulletin of the Society for the Encouragement of National Industry*.

The Discovery of Radium

Marie's next objective was her doctor's degree. In selecting a subject for her thesis, she was determined that it should involve research that was original and forward-looking.

Both the Curies were fascinated by a discovery recently made by physicist Antoine Henri Becquerel (1852–1908). Following Roentgen's discovery of X-rays in 1895, Jules Henri Poincaré (1854–1912), the mathematician, had suggested that it be determined whether such rays were emitted by fluorescent bodies under the action of light. Spurred by this suggestion, Becquerel examined the salts of uranium. He did not find what he expected. Instead he discovered that uranium salts *not* exposed to light spontaneously emitted rays of an unknown nature. A compound of uranium that had been kept in darkness for several months made an impression on a photographic plate from which it was separated by a sheet of black paper. Determining the nature of this radiation offered an opportunity for research in a virgin field worthy of a doctoral thesis.

The main problem was finding a place for Marie to work. The best Pierre could come up with was a glassed-in studio on the ground floor of the School of Physics and Chemistry. It was a storeroom for lumber and unused machines, and there was no equipment, the electrical installation was inadequate, and the room was damp and totally unsuited to scientific research. Precise instruments react unfavorably to humidity and changes in temperature, yet on February 6, 1898, Marie was forced to record a temperature of just over 43° F.

Undaunted, Marie was determined to make a go of it. Using equipment developed by Pierre and Jacques Curie in their earlier work together, she established that the intensity of radiation was proportionate to the quantity of uranium in the sample under investigation. At the same time she ascertained that the radiation was not affected by the chemical composition of the sample containing uranium, or by such external factors as light or temperature. The rays, she found, had extraordinary individuality.

The next question was whether uranium was the only body that could emit such radiation. Marie decided to examine all known chemical elements. She established that thorium also emitted the spontaneous rays, a process that she named "radioactivity." Chemical substances that were radioactive were "radio elements."

When Marie went on to measure the radioactivity of uranium and thorium, she found it a great deal stronger than was to be expected from the quantity of uranium or thorium in the samples examined. This led her to the conclusion that the samples must also contain a small quantity of a substance much more powerfully radioactive than uranium or thorium. Since she had already examined all known chemical elements, she was evidently faced by a new element. This had to be isolated.

It was then that Marie turned to her husband, and the working alliance was formed which would continue, without distinction as to who was responsible for what, until Pierre's death eight years later. Now two brains and four hands sought the unknown element.

On July 18, 1898, the Curies reported to the Academy of Sciences:

> Certain minerals containing uranium and thorium (pitchblende, chalcolite, uranite) are very active from the point of view of the emission of Becquerel rays. In a preceding communication, *one of us* showed that their activity was even

greater than that of uranium and thorium, and stated the opinion that this effect was due to some other very active substance contained in small quantity in these minerals. . . .

We believe that the substance we have extracted from pitch-blende contains a metal not yet observed, related to bismuth by its analytical properties. If the existence of this new metal is confirmed we propose to call it *polonium,* from the name of the original country of one of us.[6]

A further communication to the Academy on December 26 announced the existence in pitchblende of a second new chemical element:

The various reasons we have just enumerated lead us to believe that the new radioactive substance contains a new element to which we propose to give the name of RADIUM.

The new radioactive substance certainly contains a very strong proportion of barium; in spite of that its radioactivity is considerable. The radioactivity of radium therefore must be enormous.[7]

ISOLATING RADIUM

Today there is a growing tendency to accept scientific assumptions until they are proved wrong. Three-quarters of a century ago a greater degree of caution prevailed. Even colleagues of the Curies greeted their discovery with skepticism. The concept of spontaneous radiation emanating from radioactive bodies contradicted firmly established concepts of the composition of matter and upset theories that had for years been regarded as fundamental.

The chemists, trained to believe only in substances they had seen, touched, weighed, examined, confronted with acids, bottled, and for which they had determined an atomic weight, were less ready to be convinced than the physicists. The absence of a determined atomic weight for radium was the prime basis for rejection by the chemists.

The physicists on the other hand were vitally interested in the Curies' work and looked forward to decisive developments.

The Curies' aim was to isolate pure radium and polonium. The most highly radioactive samples they had used to date had shown only imperceptible traces of the metals they sought. Large quantities of crude material were evidently needed, but pitchblende was a costly ore, and tons of it were far beyond the Curies' financial reach. On the other hand, they knew only too well that the University of Paris or the French government would refuse any request to underwrite a purchase of pitchblende.

Pitchblende was in demand primarily for its uranium salts, which were used in the manufacture of glass. The Curies reasoned that the residue after the extraction of uranium could be of minimal value to the manufacturer. Yet that residue must contain the polonium and radium originally in the pitchblende.

The salt-extracting process was carried on at the St. Joachimsthal mines in Bohemia. The Curies asked an Austrian colleague to arrange for them to buy St. Joachimsthal residue and transport it to Paris. As it turned out, a ton of pitchblende was forwarded to them as a present from the Austrian government; the scientists had to pay only the transportation charges. Further supplies, they were informed, would be made available to them at nominal cost.

With the first shipment of pitchblende on its way, the Curies combed the numerous buildings attached to the Sorbonne looking for a suitable workshop, but without avail. They were forced to return to the little storeroom at the School of Physics and Chemistry and an abandoned shed across the courtyard from it. The skylight in the roof of the shed leaked and there was no floor. No workman would willingly have worked in the place, but the Curies were grateful for it.

Marie wrote of this period in their lives: "We had no money, no laboratory and no help in the conduct of this important and difficult task. It was like creating something out of nothing, and if Casimir Dluski once called my student years 'the heroic years of my sister-in-law's life,' I may say without exaggeration that this period was, for my husband and myself, the heroic period of our common existence. . . . And yet it was in this miserable shed that the best and happiest years of our life were spent, entirely consecrated to work. I sometimes passed the whole day stirring a mass in ebullition, with an iron rod nearly as big as myself. In the evening I was broken with fatigue."[8]

During the first of the four years (1898–1902) that the Curies worked in the shed they concentrated on the separation of radium and polonium. After a while they divided their efforts, Marie concentrating on chemical treatments designed to obtain salts of pure radium, Pierre on the properties of radium.

Radium seemed to have no intention of revealing itself for human inspection. The days of work turned into months and then years. The Curies remained undiscouraged: "At this period we were entirely absorbed by the new realm that was, thanks to an unhoped-for discovery, opening up before us. In spite of the difficulties of our working conditions, we felt very happy. Our days were spent at the laboratory. In our poor shed there reigned a great tranquillity: sometimes, as we watched over some operation, we would walk up and down, talking about work in the present and in the future; when we were cold a cup of hot tea taken near the stove comforted us. We lived in our single preoccupation as if in a dream." One day Marie asked Pierre what he thought radium would look like. "I don't know," he answered, but added, "I should like it to have a very beautiful color."[9]

Slowly the Curies gained recognition. They published papers on the discovery of induced radioactivity due to radium, on the effects of radioactivity, and on the electrical charge carried by the rays. A general report on radioactive substances, drawn up in 1900 for the Congress of Physics, aroused immense interest among European scientists.

But help was needed if they were to make progress. As early as 1898 one of the laboratory chiefs of the school, G. Bémont, had given some passing help. Toward 1900 they were joined by a young chemist, André Debierne, who went in search of a new radio element, the existence of which in the group of iron and rare clays was suspected. He discovered actinium.

About this time Pierre suggested that they abandon the search for pure radium and concentrate on radioactivity. He was apparently tiring of the seemingly endless struggle. He reckoned without Marie. She had set out to isolate radium and isolate it she would. At last in 1902, forty-five months after the Curies had announced the probable existence of radium, Marie succeeded in preparing a decigram (about one and a half grains) of pure radium in the form of one of its salts and determined its atomic weight to be 225.

At nine that night the Curies returned to the shed in the courtyard. "Don't light the lamp!" Marie said in the darkness. She added with a little laugh, "Do you remember the day when you said to me 'I should like radium to have a beautiful color'?" The reality offered more than a "beautiful color." Radium was spontaneously luminous. "In the somber shed where, in the absence of cupboards, the precious particles in their tiny glass receivers were placed on tables or on shelves nailed to the wall, their phosphorescent bluish outline gleamed, suspended in the night."[10]

Radium existed. The question now was how it would be used.

One Sunday morning in 1902 Pierre Curie told his wife: "In a few years the whole world will be wanting radium." He had, in fact, just received a letter from some technicians in Buffalo, New York, who wanted to exploit radium in America and were asking for information. "We have a choice between two solutions," Pierre continued. "We can describe the results of our research without reserve, including the process of purification. Or else we can consider ourselves to be the proprietors, the 'inventors' of radium. In this case it would be necessary, before publishing exactly how you worked to treat pitchblende, to patent the technique and assure ourselves in the way of rights over the manufacture of radium throughout the world." Marie hesitated for a matter of seconds only. The latter "is impossible," she said. "It would be contrary to the scientific spirit."[11]

The Curies had chosen forever between a fortune and relative poverty.

HARDSHIPS AND REWARDS

Through these years of investigation the Curies' struggle to make ends meet had been a hard one. Till the end of 1899 Pierre was still giving a course, involving one hundred and twenty lessons a year and direction of students' experiments, for the same five hundred francs a year he was being paid at the time of his marriage to Marie. It had sufficed then—with no children and Marie able to do housework. Irène's birth had brought the need for both a nurse and a servant. This called for an income of two or three thousand francs a year.

A simple solution would have been a professorship at the Sorbonne with its salary of ten thousand francs. Pierre obviously deserved such a post and, when a chair of physical chemistry fell vacant in 1898, he asked for it. But if he had been more politician than genius he would have known that he had little chance of getting it because he had attended neither the Polytechnic School nor the Normal School at Sèvres, near Versailles. The support that these institutions gave their former students precluded an outsider's appointment. Pierre was rejected on the dubious grounds that the discoveries he had made in the prior fifteen years were not, in the eyes of some professors, precisely in the realm of physical chemistry.

In 1900 Pierre obtained a place as tutor at the Polytechnic School. The job carried a salary of twenty-five hundred francs but was a demanding one. Then the University of Geneva offered him a chair in physics at a salary of ten thousand francs and a residence allowance. Furthermore, Marie would have an official position in his laboratory. They were tempted. The warm welcome they received when they visited Switzerland in July almost persuaded them. In the end they decided against interrupting their work on radium, an activity that could not readily be transferred to Geneva.

In October, Pierre exchanged his tiresome job at the Polytechnic for a better-paying one at the Physics, Chemistry, Natural Science Annex of the Sorbonne, and Marie was hired to lecture in physics at the Normal School. True, they were burdened with an enormous amount of additional work just when their experiments were demanding all their energy, but their budget could at last be considered balanced.

In 1902 Pierre Curie was persuaded against his better judgment to apply for membership in the Academy of Sciences. His candidacy was rejected largely, it was said, because in making his prescribed calls on the academicians he eulogized a rival candidate above himself.

He declined an offer of the Legion of Honor, indicating that what he really needed was a laboratory.

Only once during the long years did Pierre complain of the pressures to which they were subjected. "It's pretty hard," he said to Marie, "this life we have chosen."[12]

On June 25, 1903, five years after Marie had embarked on her thesis, the judges of the Faculty of Science formally announced: "The University of Paris accords you the title of doctor of physical science, with the mention 'très honorable.' " The chief judge was Professor Gabriel Lippmann, under whom she had studied at the Sorbonne. He added: "And in the name of the jury, madame, I wish to express to you all our congratulations."[13]

The honors now came fast. In June that year, when Pierre lectured at the Royal Institution in London, Mme. Curie, seated beside Lord Kelvin, was the first woman ever to be admitted to a session of the institution. In December the Curies shared the Nobel Prize in physics with Henri Becquerel. The seventy thousand gold francs that went with the prize allowed Pierre to give up his teaching. The Osiris Prize, awarded jointly to Mme. Curie and physicist Désiré Eugène

Édouard Branly (1846–1940), brought the Curies another fifty thousand francs.

In 1904 the University of Paris created a chair of physics for Pierre Curie. The appointment came too late. The professorship with its laboratory and with collaborators available had been needed during the struggling years of experimentation. It had taken the Nobel Prize and the Davy Medal, which was awarded to Pierre in London in December 1903, to get the university to act—to bestow recognition in France where the work had been done. The Curies, who for the first time in their lives had more than enough money, were bitter about this. In a lecture before a large audience at the Sorbonne, Pierre went out of his way to point out that they had done their research at the School of Physics and Chemistry of the City of Paris. He recalled with gratitude the first director of the school, who had extended himself in permitting Mme. curie to work there with him. Pierre was determined that the university should not get the credit.

LIFE AND DEATH

On December 6, 1904, a plump second daughter was born to the Curies. She was named Eve. During the pregnancy Marie had worked at the laboratory as usual and had taken only a brief respite from her teaching job. It had been a trying time, and Marie was exhausted. Eve's birth seemed to revive her. Everything interested her again—her home, her work, the events taking place in her native country, where the Poles would soon rise in support of the Russian revolution of 1905. At Eastertime in 1906 the Curie family spent several days in the country. Lying on the grass beside Marie, watching the capers of their children, Pierre murmured, "Life has been sweet with you, Marie."[14]

The following Thursday, back in Paris, Marie and Pierre went their several ways. The parting was casual. About three in the afternoon Pierre was walking along the Rue Dauphine. Absent-mindedly he stepped from behind a cab to cross the street. The cab hid an oncoming wagon drawn by two horses. When the nearer horse reared Pierre fell to the ground. Miraculously the horses did not trample him and the front wheels of the wagon avoided him. But the left rear wheel crushed the brain of Pierre Curie.

MARIE CARRIES ON

On May 13, 1906, the Faculty of Science appointed Mme. Curie to fill her late husband's place. This was the first time a woman had been offered a position in French higher education. Marie agreed to try, recalling what Pierre had said in other days: "Whatever happens, even if one of us has to go on like a body without a soul, one must work just the same."[15]

At half-past one on November 5, 1906, Marie Curie walked to her chair in the lecture hall. The applause was deafening. "When one considers the progress that has been made in physics in the past ten years, one is surprised at the advance that has taken place in our ideas concerning electricity and matter"—Mme. Curie resumed the course precisely where her husband had left off.[16]

While raising her daughters in the years that followed, Marie permitted no letdown in her work. Professor, research worker, and laboratory worker, she nonetheless continued to teach at Sèvres. She was conducting at the Sorbonne the first and, for the moment, the only course in radioactivity in the world. In 1910 she published a masterly *Traité de Radioactivité*.

In research, she was intent on the isolation of radium metal. So far her "pure radium" had been in the form of salts. Aided by André Debierne, the discoverer of actinium, she succeeded in producing the metal itself, a difficult operation that was not to be repeated for many years. Finally she developed a method, essential to therapy, of measuring radium by measuring the rays it emitted.

In 1910 she was offered the Legion of Honor. She refused it just as her husband had. A bid for membership in the Academy of Sciences was defeated by one vote. The real issue was the election of a woman.

Once again a foreign country made up for French indifference. The Swedish Academy of Science awarded Marie Curie the Nobel Prize in chemistry. This was the first time a prize was given twice to a laureate, man or woman.

In July 1914 the Institute of Radium was opened on the Rue Pierre Curie. The first steps toward such a memorial had been taken in 1909 by Pierre Paul Émile Roux, who proposed building a laboratory for Mme. Curie at the Pasteur Institute, of which he was director. This would have required Marie's leaving the Sorbonne. When word of what was planned reached the university a compromise was sought. It was finally agreed that the university and the Pasteur Institute would jointly build and finance the institute, which would provide a radioactivity laboratory (to be directed by Mme. Curie) and also a biological research laboratory in which curie-therapy for cancer would be studied.

THE WAR YEARS

Marie had rented a villa in Brittany for the summer of 1914. Irène, Eve, a governess, and a cook were already installed there. Marie, who had to remain in Paris until the end of the university year, planned to join them on August 3.

On August 2 the Germans entered France without a declaration of war. Should Marie stay in Paris or join her daughters? She decided to remain near her laboratory with the hope of preserving its delicate instruments. Actually she did not stay in Paris long. She learned that there was a job to be done in a field directly related to her own.

The discovery of X-rays nineteen years earlier had made it possible to see what was going on in the body. The military medical service had installed X-ray machines in a few big centers. But it was plain to Marie that the equipment was more needed in the field hospitals just behind the front lines. To meet this situation she equipped the first "radiological car." It was an ordinary automobile in which an X-ray machine with a dynamo driven by the car's engine was set up. Marie rode this converted vehicle from hospital to hospital. As the war intensified, more and more "little Curies," as they came to be called, were put into operation.

Marie was over fifty when the war ended in 1918. Throughout her adult life she had seen much sorrow and had unrelentingly fought one illness after another. Now she achieved a certain serenity. She knew that she would never again find the happiness that had been hers and Pierre's, but she learned to love the trifling joys of daily life.

LAST YEARS

In 1921 Mme. Curie paid a triumphal visit to America where, among other honors, President Harding presented her with a gram of radium—about as much as she had been able to accumulate in her laboratory in all her years of work—paid for by public subscription. On her return home she wrote some notes on the place of the scientist in society, a subject that was to become increasingly important through the following decades:

A great number of my friends affirm, not without valid reasons, that if Pierre Curie and I had guaranteed our rights, we should have acquired the financial means necessary to the creation of a satisfactory radium institute, without encountering the obstacles which were a handicap to both of us, and which are still a handicap for me. Nevertheless, I am still convinced that we were right.

Humanity certainly needs practical men, who get the most out of their work, and without forgetting the general good, safeguard their own interests. But humanity also needs dreamers, for whom the disinterested development of an enterprise is so captivating that it becomes impossible for them to devote their care to their own material profit.

Without the slightest doubt, these dreamers do not deserve wealth, because they do not desire it. Even so, a well-organized society should assure to such workers the efficient means of accomplishing their task, in a life freed from material care and freely consecrated to research.[17]

In 1922 thirty-five members of the Academy of Medicine submitted to their colleagues this petition: "The undersigned members think that the Academy would honor itself by electing Mme. Curie as a free associate member, in recognition of the part she took in the discovery of radium, and of a new treatment in medicine, Curie-therapy."[18] The document was revolutionary. It not only proposed electing a woman academician, but to do so without the usual presentation of candidacy. The action was a slap at the Academy of Sciences, which had rejected both Pierre and Marie Curie.

Marie continued with her work. She left for the laboratory every morning before nine and did not get home again until seven-thirty or eight. At times she was heard to exclaim, "Ah! How tired I am!"[19]

As early as 1920 she had been warned of a threatening double cataract. She was operated on four times between 1923 and 1930. She would not give in. In 1927 she wrote to her sister Bronya: "Sometimes my courage fails me and I think I ought to stop working, live in the country and devote myself to gardening. But I am held by a thousand bonds, and I don't know when I shall be able to arrange things otherwise. *Nor do I know whether, even by writing scientific books, I could live without the laboratory.*"[20]

One sunny day in May 1934 she was at the laboratory, wearily handling the tubes and apparatus that had been her faithful aids for almost forty years. At half-past three in the afternoon she said: "I have a fever and I must go home." She did not leave her bed again. On July 4 she died of "an aplastic pernicious anaemia of rapid, feverish development. The bone marrow did not react, probably because it had been injured by long accumulation of radiations."[21] Marie Curie died a victim of the radioactive substances she had discovered.

Epilogue:
Women in Medicine Today

Dr. Rosa Lee Nemir, professor of pediatrics at New York University and a leader among women doctors of the present day, sums up the attitude of many of her contemporaries when she says: "I could never have done what the women pioneers in medicine did. I couldn't have stood the sneering deprecation that Dr. Elizabeth Blackwell, the first woman physician, had to endure."[1] Fortunately the woman of today is not called upon to do so. The barriers to entering medical school, to obtaining residencies, and to embarking on medical practice have all but collapsed. Dr. Beverly C. Morgan, associate professor of pediatrics (cardiology) at the University of Washington, in her study of admissions to medical schools for the period 1929–1962 has shown that "the per cent of . . . applicants accepted is approximately equal for both sexes."[2] The era of specifically women's medical colleges ended in 1970 when the Women's Medical College of Pennsylvania became the coeducational Medical College of Pennsylvania.

The number of women entering medicine has steadily increased over the past three decades and, while the ratio of women to men is still relatively low, there are now more than 24,000 women physicians in America.

A recent study by Dr. Josephine E. Renshaw, a practicing obstetrician and gynecologist, and Miss Maryland E. Pennell of the Bureau of Health Manpower Education, covering 325,000 physicians in the United States shows that 73 percent of all actively engaged women physicians are spread over seven specialties.[3] The list is topped by pediatrics with 3632. This is hardly surprising, since the care of children is a natural for women; in fact, 20.3 percent of all physicians specializing in pediatrics are women. Psychiatry is in second place, with 2788; this, too, is not surprising, since people in distress instinctively turn to women for advice and reassurance. General practice claims 2454 women doctors; internal medicine, 2068; anesthesiology, 1461; obstetrics-gynecology, 1255; and pathology, 1164.

Only 760 women were found to specialize in surgery. This is not unexpected. Surgeons have been the last among the specialists even to consider admitting women to their sacred precincts. But this opposition is crumbling and the entrance of more women into surgery seems assured.

Turning to doctors who are engaged in activities not involving direct patient care—education, research, administration, and the like—we find that 14.3 percent of all active women M.D.s are in such pursuits, whereas only 10.3 percent of all active men are so occupied. It is on these men and women, rather than the tillers in the field, that fame and publicity more often descend.

The true evaluation of an individual's contribution can only be made by history. Attempts by peers to assess the achievements of the living can often be misleading and are rarely wholly objective. Nevertheless, among women prominent in medicine today, the following seem likely to emerge from the waiting room of history:

In pediatrics, Mary Ellen Avery for her pioneer work in pulmonary diseases; Rose Lee Nemir for her outstanding contributions to education and social organizations; Patricia Sullivan for her investigation of the development of tumors in children as a possible result of the Hiroshima bomb.

In the field of psychiatry, Katharine Wright, for opening one of the early mental-health clinics; Anna Freud, Karen Horney, and Melanie Klein for major advances in the psychiatric care of children.

Carroll Birch, hematologist, who was called to Spain to treat members of the royal family, for her contributions to tropical medicine in India and Africa; Helen Johnson for important research in hematology.

Virginia Apgar, whose basic field is anesthesiology, for developing the Apgar score, a measure for evaluating the vital functions of a newborn at sixty seconds after birth.

Elizabeth A. McGrew for her cancer research, including the development, with George N. Papanicolaou, of the *Pap smear*, a pelvic test for the detection of cancer of women.

Edith Potter, worldwide pioneer in pediatric pathology, particularly for her unique work on perinatal problems.

Leona Baumgartner for her invaluable contributions to public health with the New York City Department of Health and the Agency for International Development.

Frances Oldham Kelsey, of the Food and Drug Administration, who has earned the gratitude of countless Americans through her alertness in anticipating the detrimental side effects of thalidomide.

Kathryn Stephenson, the first woman to be certified by the American Board of Plastic Surgeons and also an outstanding author and editor.

Alma Dea Morani, the Philadelphia reconstructive surgeon of international repute, for developing, with her colleague J. Gershon-Cohen, the Panoramix, an X-ray cathode no bigger than a tongue depressor, that permits X-ray examination of such difficult areas as the bones of the face.

Helen Taussig for her surgical treatment of congenital defects of the heart.

Alice McPherson for her outstanding work in the treatment of retinal detachment.

Maude Sly for her investigations of cancer, through which she showed the relationship between resistance to malignancy and heredity.

What of the future of women in medicine?

In December 1968 Alice D. Chenoweth, retiring president of the

American Medical Women's Association, posed these questions in her message to the association: "Has society's expectation of women gradually changed so that now talented women may be expected to aspire to a professional career and at the same time pursue their feminine role of wife and mother? Is it now generally believed that self-fulfillment and a substantial contribution to society are worthy goals for women?"

Replying to her own questions, she drew on remarks made by Dr. Rosemary Park, then president of Barnard College, two years earlier: "Dr. Park's thesis is that today women are at a turning point where many options are open to them. If women decide to exploit the opportunities society offers, they can have lives of variety and richness beyond that of any other generation. It is more a question of raising the sights of women than of breaching barriers, she says, for if they choose they may aspire to full participation in professional activities and economic life."[4]

Reference Notes

1. ANCIENT HEALERS—REAL AND LEGENDARY

1. Ludwig Edelstein, "The Hippocratic Oath, Text, Translation and Interpretation," *Supplements to the Bulletin of the History of Medicine,* I (1943), p. 3.
2. J. Schouten, *The Rod and the Serpent of Asklepios: Symbol of Medicine* (Amsterdam: Elsevier, 1967), p. 119.
3. Ralph H. Major, *A History of Medicine* (Springfield, Ill.: Charles C Thomas, 1954), I, 102.
4. Kate Campbell Hurd-Mead, *A History of Women in Medicine* (Haddam, Conn.: The Haddam Press, 1938), p. 33.
5. Walter Addison Jayne, *The Healing Gods of Ancient Civilizations* (New Haven: Yale University Press, 1925), p. 248.
6. F. H. Garrison, "The Use of the Caduceus in the Insignia of the Army Medical Corps," *Bulletin of the Medical Library Association,* IX, 2 (1919), p. 13.
7. John T. Bunn, "Origin of the Caduceus Motif," *Journal of the American Medical Association,* CCII, 7 (1967), pp. 163–64
8. Schouten, *op. cit.,* pp. 117–25.
9. Hurd-Mead, *op. cit.,* p. 16.
10. Christopher Marlowe, *Dr. Faustus,* lines 1312, 1314
11. Hurd-Mead, *op. cit.,* p. 45.
12. *Ibid.,* pp. 71, 93.
13. *Ibid.* p. 93.

2. WOMEN PRACTITIONERS OF THE MIDDLE AGES

1. Hurd-Mead, *A History of Women in Medicine,* pp. 127–41.
2. Cecilia C. Mettler, *History of Medicine,* ed. Fred A. Mettler (Philadelphia & Toronto: The Blakiston Company, 1947), p. 949.

3. Quoted in Hurd-Mead, *op. cit.*, p. 143.
4. Charles Singer, "The Scientific Views and Visions of Saint Hildegard (1098–1180)," *Studies in the History and Method of Science,* ed. Charles Singer (Oxford: The Clarendon Press, 1917), p. 53.
5. Lauder Brunton, "Some Women in Medicine," *Canadian Medical Association Journal,* XLVIII (January 1943), p. 61.
6. Hurd-Mead, *op. cit.,* p. 183.
7. Cited in .Mettler, *op. cit.,* p. 196.
8. Hurd-Mead, *loc. cit.*
9. Singer, *op. cit.,* p. 6.
10. James J. Walsh, *Medieval Medicine* (London: Black, 1920), p. 164.
11. Quoted in Eileen Power, "Some Women Practitioners of Medicine in the Middle Ages," *Proceedings Royal Society of Medicine, History of Medicine Section* XV, 6 (1922), p. 23.
12. *Ibid.,* p. 21.
13. *Ibid.,* p. 22.
14. *Ibid.*

3. THE SCIENCE OF MIDWIFERY

1. Quoted in Hurd-Mead, *A History of Women in Medicine,* p. 55.
2. William Goodell, *A Sketch of the Life and Writings of Louyse Bourgeois* (Philadelphia: Collins, 1876), p. 6.
3. Irving S. Cutter and Henry R. Viets, *A Short History of Midwifery* (Philadelphia: W. B. Saunders, 1964), p. 69.
4. Goodell, *op. cit.,* p. 8.
5. *Ibid.,* p. 9.
6. Quoted in Cutter and Viets, *op. cit.,* p. 75.
7. Quoted in Hurd-Mead, *op. cit.,* p. 420.
8. Miles H. Phillips, "Percival Willughby, Gentleman. A Man-Midwife of the 17th Century," Lloyd Roberts Memorial Lecture, delivered at St. Mary's Hospitals, Manchester, November 14, 1952 (Manchester, England: pamphlet, 1953), p. 4.
9. *Ibid.,* pp. 5, 6.
10. Cutter and Viets, *op. cit.,* p. 46.
11. Quoted in James H. Aveling, *English Midwives, Their History and Prospects* (London: J. A. Churchill, 1872), pp. 63–64, from *State Trials* 32 Charles II.
12. *Ibid.,* p. 64.
13. *Ibid.,* p. 76.

14. *Ibid.,* p. 61.
15. Cutter and Viets, *op. cit.,* p. 199.
16. Cited in Hurd-Mead, *op. cit.,* p. 501.
17. Quoted in Esther Pohl Lovejoy, *Women Doctors of the World* (New York: The Macmillan Company, 1957), p. 23.
18. Hurd-Mead, *op. cit.,* pp. 428–29, 501 *n.*

4. DR. BARRY

1. Alfred Swaine Taylor, *The Principles and Practice of Medical Jurisprudence* (2nd. ed. Philadelphia: H. C. Lea, 1873), II, 286.
2. Lovejoy, *Women Doctors of the World,* p. 278.
3. George Thomas, *Fifty Years of My Life* (London: Macmillan & Company, 1876), II, 96.
4. Brunton, "Some Women in Medicine," p. 61.

5. THE FIRST STEPS: DR. HUNT, DR. FOWLER, DR. CLARKE

1. Elizabeth Bass, "Pioneer Women Doctors of the South," *Journal of the American Medical Women's Association,* II, 12 (1947), p. 557.
2. *Ibid.*
3. *Ibid.*
4. Lovejoy, *Women Doctors of the World,* p. 79.
5. Bertha L. Selmon, "History of Women in Medicine," *Medical Woman's Journal,* LIII (March 1946), p. 41.
6. Carol Lopate, *Women in Medicine,* (Baltimore: Johns Hopkins University Press, 1968), p. 7.
7. Frederick Clayton Waite, *Western Reserve University Centennial History of the School of Medicine* (Cleveland: Western Reserve University Press, 1946), p. 126.
8. *Ibid.*

6. ELIZABETH BLACKWELL

1. Ruth Fox Hume, *Great Women of Medicine* (New York: Random House, 1964), p. 2.
2. Dr. Elizabeth Blackwell, *Pioneer Work in Opening the Medical Profes-*

sion to Women (London: Longmans, Green, & Company, 1895), pp. 65–66.

3. John B. Blake, "Women and Medicine in Ante-bellum America," *Bulletin of the History of Medicine,* XXXIX, 2 (1965), p. 107.

4. Lopate, *Women in Medicine,* p. 2.

5. Blackwell, *op. cit.,* pp. 20–21.

6. *Ibid.,* p. 27.

7. *Ibid.,* p. 33.

8. *Ibid.,* p. 61.

9. Brunton, "Some Women in Medicine," p. 62.

10. Mary St. John Fancourt, *They Dared to Be Doctors* (London: Longmans, Green, & Company, 1965), p. 27.

11. Quoted in Blackwell, *op. cit.,* p. 259, from Stephen Smith, "The Medical Co-education of the Sexes," *Church Union* (1892).

12. Blackwell, *op. cit.,* p. 164.

13. *Ibid.,* p. 176.

14. *Ibid.,* p. 186.

15. Hume, *op. cit.,* p. 31.

16. Waite, *Western Reserve Centennial History of the School of Medicine,* p. 126.

17. Lovejoy, *Women Doctors of the World,* p. 52.

18. Blackwell, *op. cit.,* p. 210.

19. Marie E. Zakrzewska, *A Woman's Quest,* ed. Agnes C. Vietor (New York: D. Appleton & Company, 1924), p. 211.

20. Blackwell, *op. cit.,* pp. 222–23.

21. Frederick C. Waite, "Early Medical Services of Women," *Journal of the American Medical Women's Association,* III (1948), p. 201.

22. Fancourt, *op. cit.,* p. 126.

7. Elizabeth Garrett Anderson

1. Quoted in Louisa Garrett Anderson, *Elizabeth Garrett Anderson, 1836–1917* (London: Faber & Faber, 1919), pp. 1–2.

2. *Ibid.,* p. 41.

3. *Ibid.,* pp. 42, 43.

4. Hume, *Great Women of Medicine,* p. 91.

5. Anderson, *op. cit.,* p. 44.

6. Hume, *op. cit.,* p. 93.

7. Anderson, *op. cit.,* p. 50.

8. *Ibid.,* pp. 51–52.

9. *Ibid.,* pp. 66, 67.
10. *Ibid.,* p. 84.
11. Hume, *op. cit.,* p. 104.
12. Anderson, *op. cit.,* p. 96.
13. *Ibid.*
14. *Ibid.,* p. 101.
15. *Ibid.,* p. 112.
16. *Ibid.,* p. 113.
17. *Ibid.,* p. 118.
18. Hume, *op. cit.,* p. 115.
19. Kate Campbell Hurd-Mead, "Elizabeth Garrett Anderson," *Medical World* (July, 1940), p. 407.
20. Anderson, *op. cit.,* p. 261.
21. *Ibid.,* p. 262.
22. Brunton, "Some Women in Medicine," p. 64.

8. The Battle for Recognition at Home

1. Lopate, *Women in Medicine,* p. 8.
2. Richard Harrison Shryock, "Women in American Medicine," *Journal of the American Medical Women's Association,* V, 9 (1950), p. 376.
3. *Ibid.*
4. Brunton, "Some Women in Medicine," p. 63.
5. *Ibid.*
6. Shryock, *loc. cit.*
7. Abraham Flexner, "Medical Education in the United States and Canada," *Bulletin of the Carnegie Foundation for the Advancement of Teaching,* No. 4 (1910), p. 12.
8. Lopate, *op. cit.,* p. 15; Emily White, *Medical News* (Philadelphia), August 13, 1895, cited in "A Medical-Literary Causerie: The Evolution of the Medical Woman," *Practitioner,* LVI (January–June, 1896), p. 292.
9. Lopate, *loc. cit;* Flexner, *op. cit.* p. 6; Bass, "Pioneer Women Doctors of the South," p. 556.
10. Flexner, *op. cit.,* p. 179.
11. Shryock, *op. cit.,* p. 375.
12. Catharine Macfarlane, "Women Physicians and the Medical Societies," *Transactions & Studies of the College of Physicians of Philadelphia,* 4th ser., XXVI (1960), p. 81.
13. Quoted in *Familiar Medical Quotations,* ed. Maurice B. Strauss (Bos-

ton: Little Brown, 1968), p. 662, from *Transactions of the American Medical Association,* XXII, 17 (1871).

14. Morris Fishbein, *The History of the American Medical Association* (Philadelphia: W. B. Saunders, 1947), p. 77.
15. Quoted in Macfarlane, *op. cit.,* p. 80.
16. *Ibid.,* pp. 81–82.
17. *Ibid.* p. 82.
18. *Ibid.*

9. PROGRESS TOWARD EQUALITY ABROAD

1. Brunton, "Some Women in Medicine," p. 64.
2. "A Medico-Literary Causerie," p. 408.
3. Brunton, *loc. cit.*
4. "A Medico-Literary Causerie," p. 290.
5. *Ibid.,* p. 288.

10. MARY PUTNAM JACOBI

1. Victor Robinson, "Mary Putnam Jacobi," *Medical Life,* XXXV, 7 (1928), pp. 336–37, 338.
2. Hume, *Great Women of Medicine,* p. 176. *See also* Robinson, *op. cit.,* p. 339.
3. Robinson, *op. cit.,* pp. 343–44.
4. *Familiar Medical Quotations,* p. 662.
5. Robinson, *op. cit.,* p. 345.
6. *Ibid.,* p. 346.
7. *Ibid.,* pp. 346–47.
8. *In Memory of Mary Putnam Jacobi* (New York: Academy of Medicine, 1907), pp. 4, 5–6, 19–20.
9. Quoted in Robinson, *op. cit.,* pp. 353.

11. EMILY DUNNING BARRINGER

1. Emily Dunning Barringer, *Bowery to Bellevue, The Story of New York's First Woman Ambulance Surgeon* (New York: W. W. Norton & Company, 1950), p. 25.

2. Quoted in Iris Noble, *First Woman Ambulance Surgeon—Emily Barringer* (New York: Julian Messner, 1962), pp. 22–23.
3. Barringer, *op. cit.,* p. 41.
4. *Ibid.,* p. 44.
5. *Ibid.,* p. 53.
6. *Ibid.,* p. 70.
7. *Ibid.,* p. 76.
8. *Ibid.,* p. 77.
9. *Ibid.*
10. *Ibid.,* p. 134.
11. *Ibid.,* p. 146.
12. *Ibid.,* p. 158.
13. *Ibid.,* p. 259.

12. ALICE HAMILTON

1. Alice Hamilton, *Exploring the Dangerous Trades: The Autobiography of Alice Hamilton, M.D.* (Boston: Little, Brown & Company, 1943), pp. 29–30.
2. *Ibid.,* p. 38.
3. *Ibid.,* p. 44.
4. *Ibid.,* p. 69.
5. *Ibid.,* p. 115.
6. *Ibid.,* p. 127.
7. *Ibid.,* pp. 245–46.
8. Quoted in Joseph J. Elia, Jr., "Alice Hamilton—1869–1970," *New England Journal of Medicine,* CCLXXXIII, 18 (1970), p. 994.

13. NURSING—FROM NUNS TO NIGHTINGALE

1. Minnie Goodnow, *Outlines of Nursing History* (5th ed. Philadelphia & London: W. B. Saunders Company, 1933), p. 24.
2. Quoted in M. Adelaide Nutting and Lavinia L. Dock, *A History of Nursing,* 4 vols. (New York & London: G. P. Putnam's Sons, 1907–1912), I, 32.
3. Quoted in Goodnow, *op. cit.,* pp. 25–26.
4. Quoted in Nutting and Dock, *op. cit.,* I, p. 44, from Edward Upham, *The Sacred Books of Ceylon.*
5. Nutting and Dock, *op. cit.,* I, p. 101.

6. *Ibid.,* I, pp. 296–97.
7. Quoted in *ibid.,* I, p. 292.
8. Hurd-Mead, *A History of Women in Medicine,* p. 210*n.*
9. Quoted in Nutting and Dock, *op. cit.,* I, p. 175*n.*
10. Hurd-Mead, *op. cit.,* p. 231.
11. Nutting and Dock, *op. cit.,* pp. 499–502.
12. Goodnow, *op. cit.,* pp. 57–58.
13. *Ibid.,* p. 59.
14. *Ibid.,* p. 63.
15. *Ibid.,* p. 75

14. FLORENCE NIGHTINGALE

1. Hume, *Great Women of Medicine,* p. 50.
2. Cecil Woodham-Smith, *Florence Nightingale, 1820–1910* (New York, London, Toronto: McGraw-Hill Book Company, 1951), p. 34.
3. *Ibid.,* p. 38.
4. *Ibid.,* pp. 54–55.
5. *Ibid.,* p. 61.
6. G. E. W. Wolstenholme, "Florence Nightingale: New Lamps for Old," *Proceedings of Royal Society of Medicine,* LXIII (December, 1970), p. 1283.
7. Woodham-Smith, *op. cit.,* pp. 87–88.
8. *Ibid.,* p. 90.
9. *Ibid.,* p. 92.
10. *Ibid.,* pp. 95–96.
11. Hume, *op. cit.,* pp. 64–65.
12. *Ibid.,* pp. 65–66.
13. Woodham-Smith, *op. cit.,* p. 142.
14. Hume, *op. cit.,* p. 67.
15. *Ibid.,* p. 71.
16. Woodham-Smith, *op. cit.,* p. 222.
17. *Ibid.,* pp. 222, 247.
18. Wolstenholme, *op. cit.,* p. 1284.
19. Goodnow, *Outlines of Nursing History,* p. 108.

15. DOROTHEA LYNDE DIX

1. Helen E. Marshall, *Dorothea Dix, Forgotten Samaritan* (Chapel Hill:

The University of North Carolina Press, 1937), p. 6.
2. *Ibid.*, p. 17.
3. *Ibid.*, p. 21.
4. Quoted in *ibid.*, p. 62.
5. Dorothea Lynde Dix, "Memorial to the Legislature of Massachusetts," *Old South Leaflets*, VI, No. 148 (1843), pp. 2, 6.
6. Marshall, *op. cit.*, pp. 89–90.
7. Dix, *op. cit.*, p. 2.
8. Marshall, *op. cit.*, p. 93.
9. Franklin B. Sanborn, *Memoirs of Pliny Earle* (Boston: Damrell & Upham, 1898), p. 367.
10. Marshall, *op. cit.*, p. 100.
11. Quoted in *ibid.*, pp. 150–51.
12. Quoted in *ibid.*, p. 158.
13. Quoted in *ibid.*, p. 162.
14. Quoted in *ibid.*, p. 181.
15. Quoted in *ibid.*, pp. 182–83.
16. Quoted in *ibid.*, p. 231.
17. Quoted in Seth Curtis Beach, *Daughters of the Puritans* (Boston: American Unitarian Association, 1905), p. 161.
18. Steward H. Holbrook, *Lost Men of History* (New York: The Macmillan Company, 1946), pp. 129, 142.

16. JANE ADDAMS

1. Jane Addams, *Twenty Years at Hull-House, with Autobiographical Notes* (New York: The Macmillan Company, 1929), p. 3.
2. *Ibid.*, p. 49.
3. *Ibid.*, p. 65.
4. *Ibid.*, pp. 66, 68–69.
5. *Ibid.*, p. 85.
6. *Ibid.*, pp. 125–27.
7. *Ibid.*, p. 90.
8. *Ibid.*, p. 94.
9. *Ibid.*, pp. 125, 127.
10. *Ibid.*, p. 112.
11. *Ibid.*, p. 298.

17. MARIE CURIE

1. Eve Curie, *Madame Curie,* translated by Vincent Sheean (New York: Doubleday, Doran, & Company, 1937), p. 70.
2. *Ibid.,* p. 98.
3. Quoted in *ibid.,* pp. 120–21.
4. Quoted in *ibid.,* p. 125.
5. *Ibid.,* p. 137.
6. Quoted in *ibid.,* pp. 160–61.
7. Quoted in *ibid.,* p. 164.
8. Quoted in *ibid.,* p. 169.
9. Quoted in *ibid.,* pp. 170–71.
10. *Ibid.,* pp. 176–77.
11. *Ibid.,* pp. 203–204.
12. *Ibid.,* p. 191.
13. *Ibid.,* p. 202.
14. *Ibid.,* p. 242.
15. *Ibid.,* p. 254.
16. *Ibid.,* p. 259.
17. *Ibid.,* p. 336.
18. *Ibid.,* p. 345.
19. *Ibid.,* p. 355.
20. Quoted in *ibid.,* p. 373.
21. *Ibid.,* pp. 379, 384.

EPILOGUE: WOMEN IN MEDICINE TODAY

1. Bird, Caroline, with Sarah Welles Briller, *Born Female: The High Cost of Keeping Women Down,* (New York: David McKay Company, 1968), p. 109.
2. Beverly C. Morgan, "Admission of Women into Medical Schools in the United States: Current Status," *The Woman Physician,* XXVI, 6 (1971), p. 305.
3. Josephine E. Renshaw and Maryland Y. Pennell, "Distribution of Women Physicians, 1969," *The Woman Physician,* XXVI, 4 (1971), pp. 187–91, 195.
4. Alice D. Chenoweth, "Women in Medicine," *Journal of the American Medical Women's Association,* XXIII, 12 (1968), p. 1139.

Selected Bibliography

ADDAMS, JANE. *Twenty Years at Hull-House, with Autobiographical Notes.* New York: The Macmillan Company, 1929.

ANDERSON, LOUISA GARRETT. *Elizabeth Garrett Anderson, 1836–1917.* London: Faber & Faber, Ltd., 1936.

AUSTIN, ANNE L. *History of Nursing Source Book.* New York: G. P. Putnam's Sons, 1957.

AVELING, JAMES H. *English Midwives, Their History and Prospects.* London: J. A. Churchill, 1872.

BARRINGER, EMILY DUNNING. *Bowery to Bellevue, The Story of New York's First Woman Ambulance Surgeon.* New York: W. W. Norton & Company, 1950.

BASS, ELIZABETH. "Pioneer Women Doctors of the South," *Journal of the American Medical Women's Association,* II, 12 (1947) 556–60.

BLACKWELL, ELIZABETH. *Pioneer Work in Opening the Medical Profession to Women.* London: Longmans, Green, & Company, 1895.

BLAKE, JOHN B. "Women and Medicine in Ante-bellum America," *Bulletin of the History of Medicine,* XXXIX, 2 (1965) 99–123.

BRUNTON, LAUDER. "Some Women in Medicine," *Canadian Medical Association Journal,* XLVIII (1943) 60–65.

COOK, EDWARD. *The Life of Florence Nightingale.* 2 vols. London: Macmillan & Company, 1913.

CURIE, EVE. *Madame Curie.* Translated by Vincent Sheean. New York: Doubleday, Doran, & Company, 1937.

CUTTER, IRVING S., and VIETS, HENRY R. *A Short History of Midwifery.* Philadelphia: W. B. Saunders Company, 1964.

FLEXNER, ABRAHAM. "Medical Education in the United States and Canada," *Bulletin of the Carnegie Foundation for the Advancement of Teaching,* No. 4 (1910).

GOODELL, WILLIAM. *A Sketch of the Life and Writings of Louyse Bourgeois.* Philadelphia: Collins, 1876.

GOODNOW, MINNIE. *Outlines of Nursing History.* 5th ed. Philadelphia & London: W. B. Saunders Company, 1933.

HAMILTON, ALICE. *Exploring the Dangerous Trades: The Autobiography of Alice Hamilton, M.D.* Boston: Little, Brown & Company, 1943.

HUME, RUTH FOX. *Great Women in Medicine.* New York: Random House, 1964.

HURD-MEAD, KATE CAMPBELL. *A History of Women in Medicine.* Haddam, Conn.: The Haddam Press, 1938.

KAPLAN, HAROLD I. "Women Physicians," *The New Physician,* XX, 1 (1971) 11–19.

KERENYI, C. *Asklepios, Archetypal Image of the Physician's Existence.* Trans. Ralph Manheim. New York: Pantheon Books, for Bollingen Foundation, 1959.

LOPATE, CAROL. *Women in Medicine.* Baltimore: Johns Hopkins University Press, 1968.

LOVEJOY, ESTHER POHL. *Women Doctors of the World.* New York: The Macmillan Company, 1957.

MACFARLANE, CATHARINE. "Women Physicians and the Medical Societies." *Transactions & Studies of the College of Physicians of Philadelphia,* 4th ser., XXVI (1960) 80–83.

MARSHALL, HELEN E. *Dorothea Dix, Forgotten Samaritan.* Chapel Hill: The University of North Carolina Press, 1937.

"A Medico-Literary Causerie: The Evolution of the Medical Woman," *Practitioner,* LVI (January–June, 1896) 288–92, 407–12.

NUTTING, M. ADELAIDE, AND DOCK, LAVINIA L. *A History of Nursing.* 4 vols. New York & London: G. P. Putnam's Sons, 1907–1912.

PHILLIPS, MILES H. "Percival Willughby, Gentlemen: A Man-Midwife of the 17th Century." Lloyd Roberts Memorial Lecture, delivered at St.Mary's Hospitals, Manchester, on 14th November, 1952. Manchester, England, pamphlet, 1953.

POWER, EILEEN. "Some Women Practitioners of Medicine in the Middle Ages," *Proceedings of the Royal Society of Medicine, History of Medicine Section,* XV, 6 (1922) 20–23.

ROBINSON, VICTOR. "Mary Putnam Jacobi," *Medical Life,* XXXV, 7 (1928) 334–53.

SCHOUTEN, J. *The Rod and the Serpent of Asklepios: Symbol of Medicine.* Amsterdam: Elsevier, 1967.

SHRYOCK, RICHARD HARRISON. "Women in American Medicine," *Journal of the American Medical Women's Association,* V, 9 (1950) 371–79.

SINGER, CHARLES, "The Scientific Views and Visions of Saint Hildegard (1098–1180)," *Studies in the History and Method of Science.* Ed. Charles Singer. Oxford: The Clarendon Press, 1917, pp. 1–55.

THE WOMEN'S MEDICAL ASSOCIATION OF NEW YORK CITY, ED. *Mary Putnam Jacobi, M.D., A Pathfinder in Medicine, with Selections from Her Writings and a Complete Bibliography.* New York & London: G. P. Putnam's Sons, 1925.

WOODHAM-SMITH, CECIL. *Florence Nightingale, 1820-1910.* New York, London, Toronto: McGraw-Hill Book Company, 1951.

Illustration Credits

PAGES 11, 12, 13: M. Adelaide Nutting and Lavinia L. Dock, *A History of Nursing*. New York: Putnam, 1907. PAGE 14: Marcel Baudouin, *Femmes Médecins d'Autrefois*. Paris: Institut International de Bibliographie, 1901. PAGE 15: Hermann Fisher, *Die Heilige Hildegard von Bingen*. Munich: Verlag der Münchner Drucke, 1927. PAGES 16, 30, 31 (bottom), 33: N.U.M.L. Portrait Collection. PAGE 17: Melina Lipinska, *Les Femmes et le Progrès des Sciences Médicales*. Paris: Masson, 1930. PAGE 18: Fred. Oudschans Dentz, "Het Mysterie van den 'Kapokdokter' James Barry, die een vrouw was," *Nederlandsch Tijdschrift voor Geneeskunde* 85 (1941): 3251. PAGES 19, 21: Elise S. L'Esperance, "Influence of the New York Infirmary on Women in Medicine," *Journal of the American Medical Women's Assocation* 4 (1949): 256, 257, 259. PAGE 20: Grace E. Rochford, "The New England Hospital for Women and Children," *Journal of the American Women's Medical Association* 5 (1950): 498. PAGES 22, 24: Louise Garrett Anderson, *Elizabeth Garrett Anderson, 1836–1917*. London: Faber and Faber, 1939. PAGE 23: Margaret Castex Sturgis, "Ann Preston: Physician," *Journal of the American Medical Women's Association* 3 (1948): 509. PAGE 25: Michele Medici, *Elogio di Giovanni e di Anna Morandi Mahzolini*. Bologna: San Tommaso d'Aquino, 1851. PAGE 26: Victor Robinson, "Mary Putnam Jacobi," *Medical Life* 35 (1928): 349. PAGE 27: Léon Binet and Pierre Vallery-Radot, *La Faculté de Médecine de Paris*. Paris: Masson, 1952. PAGE 28: Emily D. Barringer, *Bowery to Bellevue: The Story of New York's First Woman Ambulance Surgeon*. New York: Norton, 1950. PAGE 29: "Who's Who in I. M. & S: Alice Hamilton," *Industrial Medicine* 4 (1935): 421. PAGE 31 (top): Clarence O. Cheney, "Dorothea Lynde Dix," *American Journal of Psychiatry* 100 (1944): 61. PAGE 32: Jane Addams, *Twenty Years at Hull-House*. New York: Macmillan, 1929.

Index of Persons

235

About the Authors

Geoffrey Marks was born in Australia and received his B.A. (1928) and his M.A. (1940) from Trinity College, Oxford. Now a United States citizen, he was formerly associate editor of Physicians' Management *and is a frequent contributor to medical periodicals, as well as the author of* The Medieval Plague *and* The Amazing Stethoscope.

William K. Beatty was born in Canada and received his B.A. (1951) and his M.S. (1952) from Columbia University. Since 1962 he has been librarian and professor of medical bibliography at Northwestern University Medical School. He has written articles for library and medical journals and contributed to books published in this country and in England. Mr. Marks and Mr. Beatty are also co-authors of The Medical Garden.